Life's Not Always a Day at the Beach

A Memoir

By Diane M. Sullivan

with Michael L. Coyne

Amy Dimitriadis and
Kathryn Villare

Copyright © 2017 Diane Sullivan
All rights reserved
First Edition

PAGE PUBLISHING, INC.
New York, NY

First originally published by Page Publishing, Inc. 2017

ISBN 978-1-64082-336-5 (Paperback)

Printed in the United States of America

My MSL Family

Acknowledgements

With special thanks to
Laura Lussier and M. Kathryn Villare
without whom there would be
no book or *The Shadow Fund NE*.

Also, with heartfelt thanks to
Lawrence R. Velvel, Michael L. Coyne,
Paula Kaldis and all my colleagues
at *The Massachusetts School of Law
at Andover.*

All proceeds from the sale of this book benefit
The Shadow Fund NE
Helping companion animals obtain
necessary medical care.

Content

	FOREWORD	
Prologue	LETTER TO DAD	I
Chapter 1	THE DISEASE AND ANDRE'S YOGURT	1
Chapter 2	REFLECTING BACK: TOP O' THE MORNING TO US	15
Chapter 3	THE EARLY YEARS	29
Chapter 4	THE DREAM OF BECOMING A LAWYER	45
Chapter 5	TRANSITION FROM STUDENT TO PROFESSOR	57
Chapter 6	MSL'S TELEVISION SHOWS	77
Chapter 7	TV TRIPS WORTH MENTIONING	83
Chapter 8	THE ANIMAL ADVOCATE	113
Chapter 9	THE FLOOD	121
Chapter 10	THE GREAT LAND GRAB	125
Chapter 11	THE BOSTON MARATHON	131
Chapter 12	THE HOCKEY AUNT	135
Chapter 13	KATHY THE PRODUCER - AUSTIN THE STUDENT	147
Chapter 14	THE BIGGEST CHALLENGE OF ALL: THE STEM CELL TRANSPLANT PROCESS	151
Chapter 15	THE BLIZZARD OF 2013	187
Chapter 16	SIX MONTHS LATER	191
Chapter 17	LESSONS LEARNED FROM THE STEM CELL TRANSPLANT - MY JOURNAL	199
Chapter 18	EPILOGUE	201
	APPENDIX	i

**With WBZ Radio's Dan Rea
at *MSL's Alumni Golf Tournament*
which benefits *The Shadow Fund NE***

Foreword

By Dan Rea
Veteran Boston television journalist, and the Host of *NightSide* on
WBZ News Radio 1030

    Diane Sullivan is an inspiration to me and I want to tell you why! Diane is one of the most unselfish and most courageous people I have ever met.

    To understand an exceptional life at so many levels, you will do no better than to peruse the pages of the book that you now hold in your hands. The title "Life's Not Always a Day at the Beach" is an understatement for sure. Diane has never sought center stage. Yet the center stage is where Diane has lived her remarkable life. I first met Diane several years ago through a mutual friend, Denise Eddy, a student at *The Massachusetts School of Law* (MSL) and a loyal listener to my nightly talk show, NightSide, on WBZ Radio. I soon was invited to help support the Shadow Fund, a charity founded by Diane to provide necessary veterinary care for the pets of people unable to provide such care for their companion animals. Unlike any other charity that I know, every penny raised or donated to *The Shadow Fund NE* helps care for people's pets. Diane runs the charity, with some help from MSL colleagues, making sure there are no administrative costs for anything. *The Shadow Fund NE* is Diane's labor of love.

    This is all done in the context of a very busy life of an Assistant Law School Dean, a Law Professor dedicated to her students' development and a very serious illness that somehow Diane will overcome.

    I have worked in the media for decades and I have won a handful of awards. So imagine my surprise when I learned that Diane Sullivan has produced hundreds of television programs that have captured not dozens, not scores but hundreds of awards – four hundred and thirty-seven to be exact.

    This is a story of challenges faced and obstacles overcome. A story of a woman, who refused to be denied a top position in a male dominated industry. The story of never surrendering whatever the odds and a story of always being concerned about others, sometimes at the expense of yourself.

    As I suggested earlier, look up the words unselfish and courageous in any dictionary and know that those two words define Diane Sullivan. It is true that despite all that Diane has achieved her "Life's Not Always (been) a Day at the Beach".

    But if I ever found myself in shark invested waters, as a lawyer in court, a law student in a classroom or a media personality on deadline, I could find no more loyal colleague and better friend that Diane. I hope you enjoy Diane's remarkable life adventure in a memoir that is sure to challenge and inspire.

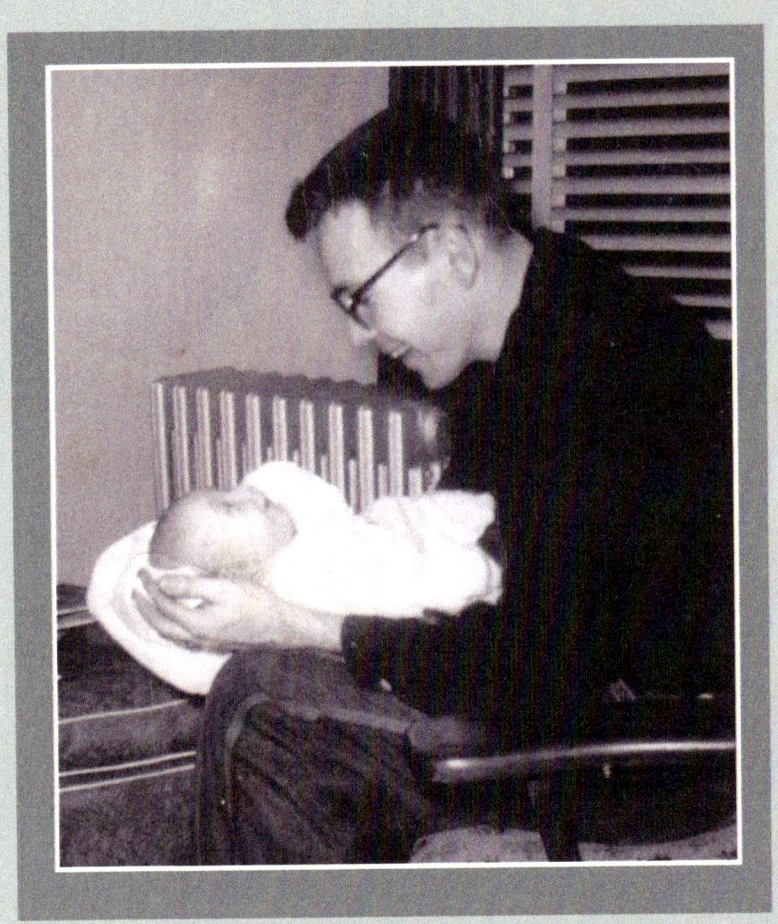

Dad and I

PROLOGUE LETTER TO DAD

Sorry it has taken me so long to write you this letter, but the words do not come easy. Nevertheless, it is long overdue. The time has come for me to say what is on my mind and in my heart.

Being the oldest child, I was the first in our family to go to college. You had only a high school education and mom did not even have that - - because when you grow up in an orphanage at age 16 you are given $20.00 and told the time has come for you to work and make your own way in the world. In neither your, or mom's case, was there money for education, so you both went to work in the factories in the City of Fitchburg. A few years later, you met, fell in love, married and I was born.

Dad, you worked most of your life, 60 hours a week in that hot paper mill for your family, and I wonder if I

Mom, Dad and Me

PROLOGUE - LETTER TO DAD

ever thanked you. The mill gave you a watch for 40 years of an exemplary work record, but did your family ever give you the pat on the back you so deserved?

I think we had little in my early years, but I felt we had everything. I thought we were rich. We had only one car, but you would get up at 4:00 a.m. instead of 5:00 a.m. and walk to work so mom and I would have the car. We would pick you up when the 4:00 p.m. whistle blew so we could eat as a family and then after you were assured our homework was done, you would return to the factory for some much needed overtime. I find it ironic how much you valued education, never having the opportunity for it yourself. Thanks dad.

When my brother John was born, you were so excited. He was your first son. How was it that you never became bitter when due to a grievous medical error, John – your namesake – was left brain damaged and mentally retarded? Instead of being angry, you made the best of a very bad situation and became a key advocate for the retarded. If you weren't at the Courthouse helping a family, you were volunteering your time at a local workshop for the mentally challenged. John now has a great life. Thanks dad.

When I was 14, you and mom had my sister Nancy. She was a bit of a challenge since the two of you were no longer kids, and she was one spirited young girl, but I really thought brother Michael, who arrived when you were age 46 and mom age 44, would put you over the edge. I was wrong. That little bundle of energy – your son and my brother Mike – became your best friend. You continued to work long hours - but said no more late nights. You told your bosses you "had" to play ball with Mike. Somehow, the money took care of itself.

Dad and I at Michael's Wedding

Dad with Ryan and Korey

PROLOGUE - LETTER TO DAD

Tragedy struck a few years later. Mom, a severe diabetic, lost her leg, and then a few years later, the second leg. She fought for her life for over a year. You became her caretaker all the while taking over her role as homemaker and mom for her two younger children. You did it all. Never bitter. Always a joke, always a smile. Thanks dad.

When mom died, you carried on. Then you fought your own battle with cancer that ultimately claimed your life. It was and still is a great loss.

Dad, I wonder if you realized what a role model you were to me and how lucky I was that you were my father. Did you ever realize back then that your hard work, sense of humor, kindness, loyalty, and courage would inspire me? Remember when I gave you those purple bell-bottoms for father's day and made you wear them to Church? I only later realized that was why we went to the 6:00 a.m. mass. But you wore them dad, so thank you.

Well, dad, did you know back then I would be a law professor and Mike would be a business professor? That three of your children would all hold advanced degrees? Nancy's two boys, the apples of your eyes, are nearly all grown up now. They play the hockey you taught them, continue to eat the "trees" (broccoli) you cooked them, and miss you more than you'll ever know. You led by example. Thanks dad.

You were the only person I ever knew who literally stopped the car and got out to help an elderly person cross the street. You brought home homeless people for meals and picked up anyone you saw walking that appeared to need a ride, all to mom's dismay. Thanks dad.

Life's Not Always a Day at the Beach

We were the only kids I knew that had to stand in the living room when the national anthem played. I though back then it was too extreme. Now, I thank you for instilling pride and respect and gratitude, a sense of national pride. Thanks dad.

How fitting it is that each year all of your family attends the annual Jack & Lou Leamy scholarship fund event in your honor. How appropriate it is that your son, a professor at Fitchburg State, awards a scholarship to a local kid attending Fitchburg State University. Remember how you encouraged me to attend night school at Fitchburg State College? Well, you were the smart one. Thanks dad.

You told me you can be anything you dream to be – provided you are willing to work hard. "Dream big," you said and we did. Even your grandsons think they are heading to the NHL - - just like Mike thought he was going to the Red Sox, and no doubt his sons will think so also. Thanks to you, none of us lack the confidence to aim for the stars.

You required us to be nice, good neighbors. I had to volunteer as a candy striper at Burbank Hospital, my siblings were required to volunteer to help the mentally retarded. You told me we had a whole lifetime to work, that we should donate our time, our first work years, and so we did. In the end we got back more than we gave. Thanks dad.

You promoted sports. How many road races and marathons did you drive us to and from, standing often times in the rain cheering us on - - even if we were dead last! Thanks dad.

PROLOGUE - LETTER TO DAD

You coached so many little leagues and donated so much to the West Fitchburg Little League. Funny thing was, you always chose kids no one else wanted on their team and you always won. All of those kids still remember you today. Thanks dad.

In the end, you were the most courageous person I have ever known. You fought hard through chemotherapy and the last nine weeks of your life were so very bad. You never complained – always hoping to get to one more of your grandson's games. Thanks dad!

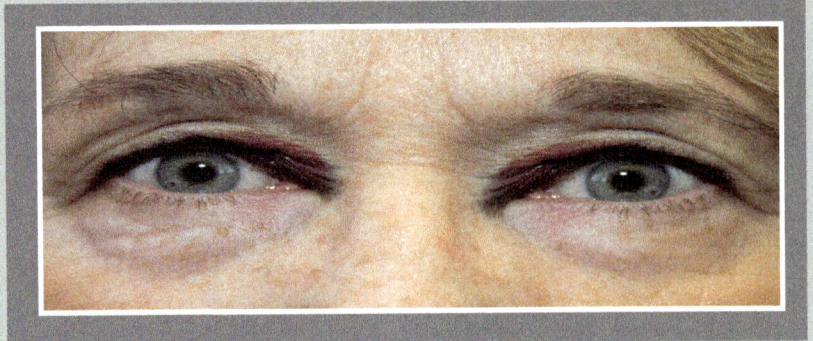

My Warrior Eyes

Boston Medical Center, Boston, MA

Andre's Cafe Boston, MA

THE DISEASE AND ANDRE'S YOGURT

My "Warrior" Eyes

This part of my story begins with my purple, warrior eyes. More often than not, I look like I have been in a fight and took the brunt of it, with bleeding and bruising around my eyes. My retina specialist was quite concerned so she ordered a biopsy, which turned out negative. However, the bruising and bleeding continued. I visited my primary care doctor's office, but the attending Doctor referred me back to my retina specialist who responded that the biopsy was negative so it must be a medical issue. The medical doctors found nothing so I ultimately ignored the fact that I looked like I took a hockey puck in the eyes.

Being Irish, I have the curse of very fair skin, so each year I visit my skin doctor to have any "pre-cancer" spots taken off. When I saw Dr. Finkle last year, after much resistance on my part, I let him biopsy my eyelid. Dr. Finkle was concerned over the bruised eyelids, but I had explained to him they had been checked, and biopsied and nothing abnormal was found. "This is just how they are," I said. "No, Diane," said Dr. Finkle, "This is not normal". "The biopsy showed nothing," I responded. "Sometimes," he said, "it depends who reads it. You are here, what's the harm? Let me biopsy your eyelids." "O.K.," I reluctantly agreed. I was in a hurry and the last one was quite painful, so I wasn't excited to repeat the procedure, but I agreed. Interestingly, it was quick and painless, and I left his office without giving it a second thought.

A few days later, my colleague, Paula Kaldis and I were meeting in my office to discuss a student issue, when the front office buzzed me to say Dr. Finkle was on the phone for me. I took the call. It was then I heard about the disease – amyloidosis - - for the first time. And I quickly learned this was not good . . . Amyloidosis - - is a very rare disease where proteins (amyloids) are deposited into various tissues and organs of the body. In my case, I have primary "AL" Amyloidosis, which means my bone marrow is producing this abnormal protein. The bad news: there is no cure, and it will lead to organ failure. So the prognosis for a diagnosis of amyloidosis is not a good one, but the good news in my case was at least that mine was caught early before significant organ damage occurred.

Boston Medical Hospital/Boston University Medical Team

So, on this day, we came from Columbia, Israel, South Carolina, and Massachusetts - - all for the same thing - - the promise for tomorrow and next year's holidays. We want to see our children grow, walk our dogs, and do our jobs, nothing special except to continue to live our lives. Despite all the criticisms of our health care system, I realize how fortunate I am to be here today. I

Dr. David Seldin,
Dr. Vaishali Sanchorawala and I

Dr. Rosemary O'Connell and I

Life's Not Always a Day at the Beach

checked into the Boston Medical Center for my three day evaluation in August of 2011. I arrived early, wanting to put this behind me as quickly as possible. I had only a few days off from the law school before the start of the next semester.

I was greeted by the lovely, cheery, Natasha Yancy, who clearly ran the clinic's agenda. She was as efficient as she was upbeat and nice. This helped. No sense having a doom and gloom attitude. I was given a schedule consisting of tests and meetings to determine the type of amyloidosis I had, and the degree of organ involvement. I met my primary attending physician specialist within the amyloid program, Dr. Rosemary O'Connell. Given a choice, I would have chosen her to head up my care. She is also someone I would choose as a friend. I felt fortunate because I was in such good health. All medical staff, physicians, and specialists assumed I had the localized form of amyloidosis which is the best type to have because it will not kill you, but stay localized to the area region of the body it arises in. It was believed that's what my tests would show - - localized to the eye area. The medical team was so hopeful of this when they saw me, that they removed the planned bone morrow biopsy from the tests saying they would hate to put me through this if it wasn't necessary. I asked if it was localized would that be it - - Would I be fine, and was told, "yes".

As the afternoon approached, I knew I was in trouble when Natasha kept adding tests to my schedule. I was already doing a twenty-four hour urine collection when Natasha stopped me to ask for a sample for "Dr. Seldin's research". When I was told midday that the bone marrow was added, I knew then the results were not going to be good - - this would not be a localized form of amyloidosis.

THE DISEASE AND ANDRE'S YOGURT

Dr. Rhuberg, the Cardiologist assigned to assess cardiac involvement, was simply top-shelf. After examining me he said he would not be surprised if I had Primary AL. His instincts were good, as Dr. O'Connell confirmed the suspicion later that day. I have Primary AL Amyloidosis – a very rare disease affecting only 1,200 – 2,000 of us each year worldwide. The disease is probably often misdiagnosed, so the actual number of cases is anticipated to be much more.

Everyone associated with the amyloid program at Boston Medical is competent, caring, and simply outstanding. I was puzzled how this could be so. Then I met the head of the amyloidosis program, Dr. David Seldin - - smart, kind, calm, positive, great listener - - a leader who inspires. He deals in hope. I now understood why BU/Boston Medical were the leaders in the field.

Dr. Seldin made time in his schedule for me. Our conversation was brief. I had confidence in him, though I knew when he asked some general questions, and then asked about whether I had nearby family and good support - - the diagnosis and ultimate treatment plan would be worse than I hoped for.

All six of us patients gathered in the waiting room were searching for good news - hope. We all wanted to live - - see our families grow up. I know I want to see my four nephews grow up, continue working at the job I love, and caring for my two dogs whose care totally depends on me. Others in the room felt the same way.

When it was time for the bone morrow biopsy, I was not frightened in any way. Ignorance is bliss! I had a very light hearted conversation with the young female doctors, who explained they would be taking bone from

Life's Not Always a Day at the Beach

my back.

The first pressure I would feel was lidocaine, which was suppose to help numb the pain. I was totally at ease - - until the first failed attempt to get the bone sample. Nothing could have prepared me for this. One doctor said to the next, you hold her down. I thought to myself, "we stopped holding people down centuries ago". The procedure ended with me soaking wet, and in tears. It was truly horrible. The doctors said, "and you were so cool and cocky when we started." They were apologetic and kind, but the procedure was really horrible. Immediately though, as I was making my way to x-ray in the next building, I could feel that I was still sweating profusely. I began to cry, soft at first, but then uncontrollably. Medical people and passerbys' stopped. "Who is with you?" they demanded "Are you from the amyloid program? Did you have a bone marrow biopsy?" Somehow they knew!

It was then I saw the sign for Andre's - - "Best Yogurt in the World". I was drawn across the street almost against my will. I have absolutely no will power to resist frozen yogurt, and I believe in the healing power of yogurt. Andre's is not an ordinary restaurant - - the owner cares more about people than making a profit. He could see how upset I was and asked why. I explained that I was a patient at Boston Medical. He refused to take money for my order. Who does that? Every time I return to Boston Medical, I treat myself to Andre's yogurt - - you pick the ingredients and they mix it into the yogurt. When I leave Andre's, I leave behind all my troubles, or so it seems.

When the tests were all back, the findings were not as I hoped; 15% to 20% of my bone marrow had the disease, it was in my tissues, and ultimately I would need

"Best Yogurt in the World"
Andre's Cafe, Boston, MA
(Got me through the worst of times)

Life's Not Always a Day at the Beach

aggressive treatment. It appeared I would be a good candidate for an autologous (using my own cells) stem cell transplant with high dose melphalan (chemotherapy).

If the autologous stem cell transplant works, I could have a durable remission – hopefully long enough to outlive my dogs, educate my nephews, and finish my job at the law school. Less than six months later, I was not feeling well and as much as my greatest strength has always been my high energy level, I now felt all that dissipating. Medical treatment seemed a necessity.

After contacting my doctors, it was decided that the disease was progressing. I had a kidney biopsy, which admittedly I was somewhat apprehensive about. However, I was informed I'd be sedated, so this eased my fear. When I was wheeled in on the gurney, I was nervous. The doctor in charge of this procedure asked if I was nervous. I responded, "yes". "Good," he said, "only two types of patients come in - - those that are afraid and those that are stupid, and I'm not in the mood for stupid today." We laughed, and I was put at ease.

As luck would have it, due to the location of my kidneys, I could not receive a sedative because I had to be able to respond to commands, like "Hold your breath," so they could access my kidneys. So, let me say it was not my best experience, but the medical team was superb. A short time later, I began chemotherapy. All things considered, it wasn't that bad. I had a wonderful infusion nurse named Cynthia, and weekly check-ups with Dr. Seldin and Dr. O'Connell. I would bring work with me, and the time went fast. I followed each infusion with a visit to Andre's yogurt. Vanilla yogurt with granola ground in - - unbelievably good. The only thing better was having oreo cookies ground in, but by choosing granola, I can pretend

THE DISEASE AND ANDRE'S YOGURT

I am health-conscious.

The only real problem was the terrible headaches after the infusion and the inability to sleep – probably from the steroid infusion that accompanied the chemotherapy. So, although things went well and I never missed a day of work, unfortunately the chemotherapy did not work, so it was stopped in June after only approximately six months. After careful thought and deliberation upon Dr. Seldin and Dr. O'Connell's recommendations, I decided to plan for a stem cell transplant – NO small undertaking. I knew this was a risky procedure, but it would provide my best chance at a durable remission. There are, however, major obstacles: the need to be in close proximity to the hospital, which would require living in a nearby hotel for a couple of months. I live in North Andover – some 30 miles from Boston. So, what do I do about my dogs? Also, one of the rules was twenty-four hour care. Thus, I needed to figure out who could care for me, who could care for my dogs? The big risk for me was bleeding to death - - something I could not prevent. I worry, if this happens, who will take my dogs? Who will help get my nephews through college? For the first time, I can see my mortality on my radar. I intend to fight it, but reality is, I can't control whether I make it.

The first day of orientation at the law school in August of 2012, I reported in at Boston Medical for a two day check-up. I was dreading having the bone marrow taken from my back, but otherwise it all had become routine - - as routine as a serious disease can be.

When I checked in, I was somewhat surprised at how high my heart rate was. The nurse commented on this. I responded that if she was going to have bone taken from her back, her heart might also be beating fast too.

Life's Not Always a Day at the Beach

So, when Dr. O'Connell saw me it was hard to decide who was more surprised that my EKG showed an irregular heartbeat, her or I. She discussed the possibility of going to the operating room and having paddles used to restore my heartbeat. This is not good, I thought, but we agreed to cancel the bone marrow biopsy as a result of this new heart issue - - so some good did come from it, I thought. In the end the heart specialist decided to try me on a medication to regulate my heart.

I next met with the stem cell nurse to learn what would happen during this process. Dina began by telling me normally the meeting was ninety minutes to two hours. In the end, I was glad we only had fifty minutes before my next medical appointment, because I totally broke down. Interestingly, it wasn't when she opened telling me I could have no contact with animals. That would be a deal breaker for me. I asked why not, and she responded because of germs. When I asked specifically what germs were communicated she said she'd research it. I explained my doctors knew I lived with two dogs and would not leave them, so we decided we'd move onto the next set of restrictions. I would have to stay in Boston (within 15 minutes) for sixty days. I said I was told one half-hour, and my house was twenty-five minutes without traffic from Boston. Dina said she couldn't sleep at night if I didn't stay in Boston, at least during the critical period, so I knew I'd have to agree to this. She told me I had to have 24/7 care, but the good news was it didn't have to be the same person.

The funny thing was, or not so funny thing was, when she next told me I would need to have someone with me on November 5th and 6th that could get me through the ICE. I asked what this was, and she explained for a 50 minute interval ice would need to be stuffed in my

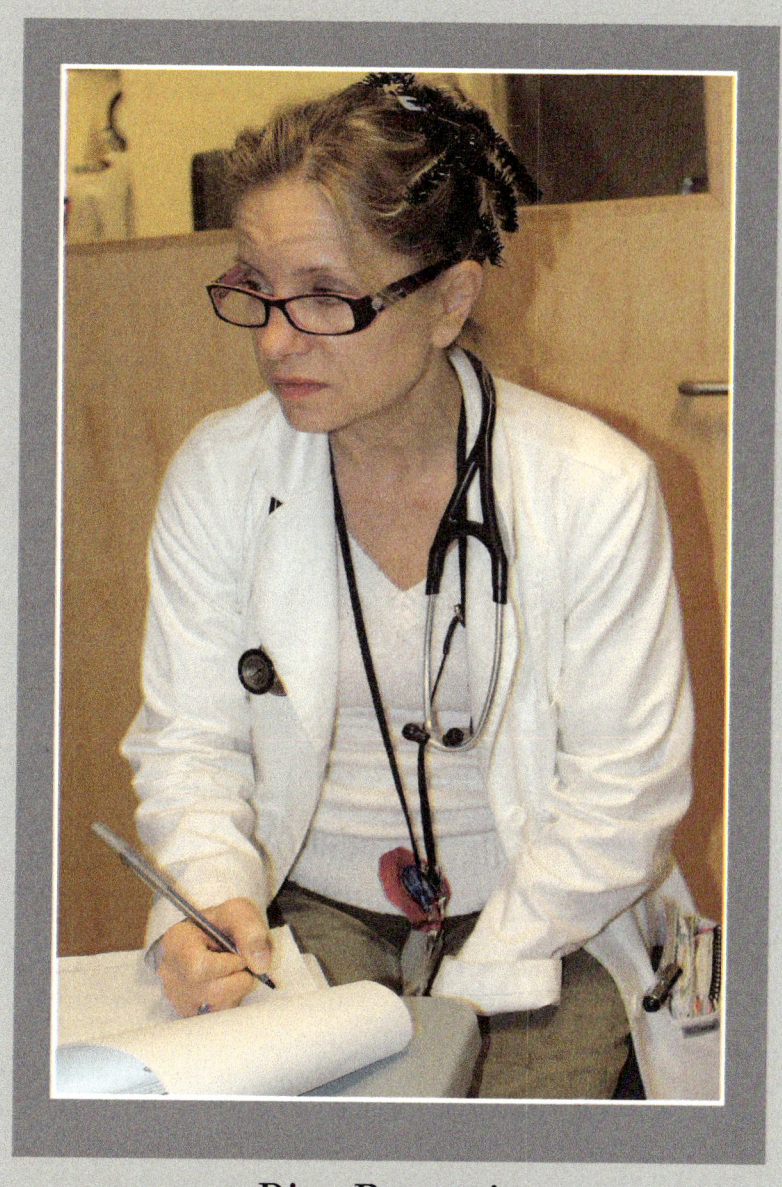

Dina Brauneis
RN, MSN, CNS, APRN, NP-C
Clinical Research/Stem Cell Transplant Nurse Practitioner, Boston Medical Center, Boston, MA

Life's Not Always a Day at the Beach

mouth and down my throat to prevent lesions. To say I began to cry was an understatement – Dina explained this is where everyone fell apart. It was the worst part she told me. I told her I could not do it. She kept saying, yes you can. Somehow Dina would always rescue me from self-doubt and if she couldn't do so, my colleague Mike Coyne could. I left her crying uncontrollably, and proceeded to sit in the waiting room and sob. It is hard to imagine with everything I was facing ICE is what got me. My brother would say it was just the final straw. No, it is the fear of feeling as if I'm suffocating with cold ice that I can't bear.

After my echocardiogram, I left for home. I was in line at the pharmacy when the call from Dr. O'Connell came. She just wanted to let me know I was being added to Dr. Seldin's schedule, and yes he was going to do the bone marrow biopsy. Yes, this day gets better and better. As the saying goes, "What doesn't kill us makes us stronger".

I did not ever contemplate considering the manner in which I would die. When Dr. Seldin explained my risk of bleeding and Dina described stuffing my mouth and throat with ice, I began to think about cancelling the stem cell transplant. I thought, I'd much prefer to work and keep going until I no longer could, and then simply die when my time was up, no big fanfare. Although, I am petrified of seeing death, I am not afraid to die. However, make no mistake: I WANT TO LIVE. DYING WAS NOT AND IS NOT AN OPTION. It is simply unthinkable to me, yet I do know I would hate to die bleeding to death. That is not a way I would chose to end my life. I do realize, however, I do not control this. So, this is why I need to leave my dogs, and home in North Andover and move to a hotel two blocks from the hospital.

THE DISEASE AND ANDRE'S YOGURT

If I start to bleed and get to the hospital right away, I have to hope the medical team can stop it. I have great confidence in my doctors, but this is like rolling the dice to me - - and I don't play cards. So, what's the option? No real good one. My latest medical test results came in, and the disease is progressing. Yesterday was the first day I almost went home from work before noon, but fortunately, I staved off the fatigue and made it through. The reality is though that I do not feel well, and I am out of options.

Whitey and Me

REFLECTING BACK: TOP O' THE MORNING TO US

God Whitey, it's not even 5:00 a.m. Must you always be so excited to start your day? Ten more minutes sleep is all I ask. After all, it is pitch dark out and our New England winters seem to be getting even more frigid as we approach the winter of our lives. No, you do not have to hunt and scrounge for your food. I'll feed you. You know I always do. Yes, I remember our deal, our secret pact - - we'll outlive each other. And yes, we must keep moving even when it is hard to do, so get me up, yank me up if you must old boy – bark at me, but never let me rest easy. I know those were my words. I'll do the same for you. If we are going to survive this, it is what we must continue to do my old friend. I know it's much harder now. Believe me, I know our struggle. Your back legs are very stiff now, mine are not any better. The walk will help us both. Who knows what adventures await.

Life's Not Always a Day at the Beach

Whitey is my eighth dog. Each one was my favorite. It was another freezing cold night when Whitey was found. Dad was dying and we were experiencing yet another severe cold spell. I didn't mind the weather because it seemed to match my mood - - icy and miserable. Mom had died five years earlier and I felt like - - even as a grown woman with three adult siblings - - I was becoming an orphan. Whitey was at a convenience store standing with the trash trembling in the cold. Gaunt, matted, and starving, he approached George's car. It was 4:00 a.m., freezing cold, and this short-haired, thin dog was looking for food at a gas station. The tattered men's tie wrapped around his neck with a rabies tag on his unmarked collar was the only clue to his identity. It was clear he had either been hit by a car or beaten because he had evidence of a blow to his head and a gash over his right eye. When my friend George inquired inside, the attendant said the dog had been hanging around there a couple of days. He thought the dog had been living in the woods behind the store for some time. He lived among the "street people," who used the old tie as a leash. He had been starving and alone for a while now. No one should live or die like that.

A few hours later, when George called me to check on Dad, he told me he could not find the owner, and if the dog checked out okay at the veterinarian's, he was thinking of keeping him. I remember thinking, "Even if the dog doesn't check out health-wise, we need to keep him" but I also thought the dog's health was the least of his problems - his cat's reaction to this dog was a bigger problem. George must have read my mind because his next question was whether I thought his cat and this dog could get along. I responded "Absolutely," knowing full well that wasn't the case. I told him to put up a divider and keep the dog and cat separated and just let them smell each other for a few days. So a gate was installed to keep the

Whitey and Hakuna

Whitey and Me

Life's Not Always a Day at the Beach

dog in the kitchen and away from the cat, but Christmas (the five-pound cat) decided to take matters into her own "paws": she promptly jumped the gate and jumped on the dog's back, digging her claws into him until he screamed. From that moment on, the dog never once bothered the cat, but I knew the bigger challenge would be when the dog arrived at my house to face my nine-year-old male chow, Hakuna. How would Hakuna, the king, react to another male dog in his home? I knew he would end up as my dog. They always were my dogs, my companions, and my friends.

We ultimately were able to track down the dog's owner through the rabies tag. He said the dog had been "a pain." His name was Churchill. He had run away a number of times. He had no use for him. I had no use for the owner.

Churchill was renamed Whitey (in part because, like Whitey Bulger, he was on the run). He weighed in at 68 pounds at the veterinarian's and received a clean bill of health. The only prescription necessary was some TLC and food. The big test, however, still was ahead: meeting Hakuna.

When Whitey came to my home a short time later, Hakuna went on full alert. A big scuffle ensued. We pulled these two alpha male dogs apart and put Whitey in a separate room with the gate. This time the gate worked; both dogs respected the boundary.

"Let's give it a little time," I thought, which was really the prayer of the hopeless. I was on overload. Dad was dying, Hakuna was angry and upset. Whitey was scared and homeless. The two dogs could sense my despair. Thank God they decided to call a truce - - if not for

REFLECTING BACK: TOP O' THE MORNING TO US

themselves, then for me.

Dad died weeks later; Hakuna and Whitey became best friends (well, almost), and we moved to our current home in North Andover. Whitey now weighed 95 pounds, and that was after his diet. Life was good for Whitey. Like most Labrador retrievers, he would get up with the sun every morning, ready to go. (That was probably a problem with his original family.) He liked his breakfast early - and in fact came to expect it -and then it was time for his hour walk. When we returned home, he would go back to bed for the morning. Unfortunately, I couldn't. So it was really good that I am an early-morning person. The first day he came to live with me, he thought 3:30 a.m. was a good time to get up. I convinced him 5:00 a.m. will have to do. At the end of the day, Whitey had his supper and a final walk before he curled up for his night's sleep. He went to bed early; after all, 5:00 a.m. comes early!

Six years ago, our dear friend and my beloved Hakuna died. After a painful period, I adopted a new companion for Whitey, a four-year-old shelter rescue named Winnie.

Winnie is a Chow Chow that was born in a puppy mill. She was taken from her mother, put in a crate and shipped north. She was then placed in a mall store window for sale at a handsome price. Looking like a little bear cub, she was bought on impulse. Mall puppies too often are. Chows can be willful, protective, loyal, and like me, her Irish adoptive mother, independent to the degree of obstinacy. At first, things worked out well for Winnie, but then the economy turned. Winnie's family became homeless. They then lived in a car because no one would rent to a family with three dogs, little money, and fewer friends. Winnie's fur became matted, the car far too crowded, and ultimately she arrived at a kill shelter.

As the days passed, Winnie became aggressive and hard to control. Winnie was in the animal shelter, and it was day 58. The clock was ticking. No one even came to look at her. Soon she would be one of the six million orphaned dogs and cats killed each year.

The shelter posted her adoptive information on the internet. Her picture and hundreds of others were there for interested families, but like Whitey and me now too, Winnie's time was rapidly drawing to a close. I was haunted by her story. However, I knew eight-year-old Whitey did not want another dog in his home. Maybe though, there was still some way we could make it work.

Whitey was not the only problem. My partner, George didn't want another dog either. He especially had no interest in an aggressive four-year-old Chow. He had less interest in a Chow in rough shape that no one else wanted and that even the shelter said could not live with another dog. But Winnie deserved to be rescued, and I needed to help, having suffered my own share of losses over the last year. We would help each other.

At the shelter, the animal behaviorist met me and asked a worker to get Winnie from her cage. Winnie was shaking and terrified. As I got down on the floor, Winnie came over and cautiously gave me a kiss. We bonded. We headed for home finding comfort in each other.

My euphoria gave way to worry. Worried about Whitey's reaction. Worried about George's reaction. George was not home when we arrived. That was a relief. I could introduce the dogs without his watchful eyes. I put Whitey outside and brought Winnie to meet her new

Winnie and Me

Life's Not Always a Day at the Beach

"brother." What a disaster! With two growling dogs both seeking supremacy, it could not have been worse. I decided to introduce the dogs by walking them together. I grabbed two leashes and away we went. Within minutes they were walking side by side getting along just fine; all happy, we turned to head for home.

Rounding the corner, I saw an unleashed Rottweiler come crashing through a closed screen door, bolt across the lawn, and barrel toward Whitey, Winnie, and me. The Rottweiler attacked. Whitey bore the brunt of it. Winnie ran for her life, darting away through oncoming traffic. A van with horn blaring, nearly crushed her. Then she was gone.

Screaming and sobbing for help, I begged bystanders to find my Winnie while I attended to Whitey. A trembling and terrified Winnie was later found. I put her in the house to head to the veterinarian with Whitey. George then arrived home to a terrified dog that he did not want. Winnie did not want him either. Growling and snarling, a frightened Winnie would not let him in the house. That day just got better and better.

George was so angry when I pulled into the driveway that I retreated to another part of the house and kept quiet. That silence was later broken when I overheard George say "O.K., Winnie, you want to give me your paw . . . and a kiss, too. Good girl." Winnie certainly was appropriately named.

So after that, Whitey, Winnie, and I got up with the sun, went for a walk in the woods, and played ball in the yard. During Winnie's first walk in the woods, she was terrified. Crossing a little brook, I had to pick her up and carry her across and when she heard a chirping bird, she stopped and trembled. Later when I put on my hiking boots, she got so excited that she jumped high in the air with delight. She led the way running over the creeks with abandon, chasing the birds away, and making her own joyous noise. Whitey, being a male, marked his territory along the way. Winnie awkwardly learned to do the same.

Our walks became more difficult with age and illness taking its toll. But we kept on going, not giving into it. Then it was just the "two of us". As Natalie Wood said, "Almost every girl falls in love with the wrong man, I suppose it's part of growing up". How right she was. Love blinds us all to the obvious character deficiencies in others. Nonetheless, George's timing could not have been worse.

I would not have chosen flying solo at this particular time in my life. This is when I most needed help. As is often the case though, we do not get to choose our moments in time, our only choice is how we respond to the things that happen. I would like to think I've made the best of what could have been a disaster. As my dear friend Mike Coyne reminds me from the teachings of Dale Carnegie, "Learn to make lemonade from lemons"!

So, I've now come to realize being alone is a victory not a failure. I have a busy job that can be very demanding. Student problems and issues, which are never in short supply can consume me at times, like today, when a young mother seeks my counsel because her toddler was sexually molested by her lover. On these days it is good to open the door and enter my home with no one there except my dogs, who are always happy to see me. They force me to take a long walk, usually in the woods, or hike up a hill to view the magnificent skyline of Boston. I am

Winnie, Whitey and Me

REFLECTING BACK: TOP O' THE MORNING TO US

at peace there - - more than any place on earth, except for my law school, or when I am with my family. When we return home, the dogs disappear and allow me to be alone to recharge.

I am not looking to be rescued or discovered. I have found I like being alone. Relationships, long term and short term, have never worked out for me. I like the silence and accomplishments of cutting grass, and shoveling the snow off the driveway. There is a certain sense of accomplishment and strength in being alone. Yes, I have lots of support from family, friends, colleagues, and neighbors. Many people would be lonely if they lived alone. I am not one of those people.

My life has balance with silence and solitude, and these are necessary ingredients in life for me. When I am in a relationship, I struggle not to lose who I am and what I care most about. Now I can relax and just be me. I can focus my energy, all of it, on whatever battle awaits me, or wherever I feel I can make a difference.

I am not feeling well right now. It is a very good thing that after a day of teaching and walking the dogs, I can dive into bed. I am focused on me. I do not have to eat or make conversation. My dogs will curl up on the floor in my bedroom. Winnie guards the entrance to my room, and Whitey beats me to sleep. This sight of my dogs is a sight I love. I am at peace. They are at peace.

Cher is right. In the end, "We all sleep alone." That thought may be unpleasant for some. I will continue my fight along life's way alone. The pictures on the wall and in my photo albums have been cleansed of the past. The only males that remain are related to me, or work with me. It's sad really, that you put so much effort into

Dogs are better than human beings because they know but do not tell.
Emily Dickinson

REFLECTING BACK: TOP O' THE MORNING TO US

a relationship - - years, even decades - - and within hours of the relationship ending every memory is removed to prevent doubt of decisions made. No regrets. I am moving on. I'll fight alone.

**My Grandfather Leo
with Aunt Mary Lou**

THE EARLY YEARS

Everyone who got to where they are had to begin where they were.
                                    Richard Paul Evans

Dad, Jack Elder, was a truly wonderful man: Kind, gentle, with a great sense of humor. He was the son of two Irish immigrants, and was the middle child. Dad was a great athlete - - football, basketball, hockey, and baseball. It is too bad he never had the opportunity to take his talents further or to go onto college, but his family had little money and none to help their middle child. Like so many kids in large urban cities like Fitchburg, dad went to work in the paper mills. His family loved sports. Dad was named Jack Elder, after Jack Elder who intercepted a pass during Notre Dame's game with the Army and returned it 100 yards for the touchdown on the day dad was born.

In my grandfather's house few things mattered

more than Notre Dame football. In fact, if Notre Dame lost a Saturday afternoon football game, my grandfather refused to eat dinner and simply went straight to bed after the game at FOUR O'CLOCK IN THE AFTERNOON. My father and his siblings did the same, thinking this was the "normal" and proper thing to do! When television sets first became available for purchase, he and his brother pooled all of their savings and purchased a television on the condition it would be installed in the home before Notre Dame's kick-off that following Saturday.

My grandfather wrote pieces for one of Notre Dame's publications which I found interesting, since no one in my family before me had ever been to college. He also appeared regularly as a featured guest on a sports radio show under a pseudo name. I was nearly twenty years old before I knew the man I loved to listen to on 1280 AM was really my grandfather.

Dad was kind but you had better be fair — or a square shooter when dealing with him. One time when dad was a young man he was out at a neighborhood bar when the owner asked him to fight some other young man, as the two were excellent boxers. The agreement was they would just spar a few rounds and split the money the owner would pay them, but when the crowd roared his opponent decided to go for it all with a blow to dad's head. Dad got up and proceeded to knock this guy out. He then took the money, split it in half giving his unconscious opponent's share to the bartender, telling him drinks on the house for everyone in attendance.

Mom's life was very different. She was one of four children, three girls and a boy. Their father abandoned the family when they were young children and later died in an automobile accident 1,000 miles away. Her mother

**Dad at
Rockefeller Center
New York
1953**

**Mom at
McTaggarts Pond
Fitchburg, MA
1953**

Life's Not Always a Day at the Beach

---

later. Nothing was more important to mom than family. Absolutely nothing.

My parents loved and adored me, and I was a very happy child. My brother, John was born 3 1/2 years after me. As an infant, he developed a respiratory infection that required him to be placed in an oxygen tent. When they put my cute, adorable infant brother inside, the medical team connected it incorrectly and John was left brain damaged and disabled.

Mom and Dad were Catholics and we were parishioners at Sacred Heart Church which sat on top of a hill in West Fitchburg. West Fitchburg was the part of the city where the Irish lived, so it was only natural I attended the companion catholic school. My first few grades went well - - I liked school, spelling, math, and had very good grades.

When John turned six, he was enrolled in the same catholic school I was attending. It was a disaster! Instead of punishing John when the nuns felt he didn't measure up, they punished me for his lack of intellectual ability or misdeeds. It wasn't long before John was transferred to special education classes at the public school and my relationship with the nuns improved — but not for long.

By this time in my life I was already a vegetarian. Our family used to visit Coggshall Park — a true oasis within the city limits — to feed the ducks, swans and geese. It didn't take long for me to make the connection that these "large birds" resembled the turkey carcasses in the meat department cases of the local supermarket. Once the connection was made, I never ate a piece of meat again, much to the constant criticism of my paternal grandmother. What is interesting is that John was also

**Dad and Mom - Whalom Park
Lunenburg, Massachusetts**

**Dad and Mom - White Cross Trail,
Mount Monadnock, NH - 1953**

Life's Not Always a Day at the Beach

barely cared for her children. They were often found wandering the streets dirty and hungry, and were placed in an orphanage when she was about seven. The worst part of that was that her brother, Robert who was four years old when they were surrendered to the orphanage, had to live in a separate building from his sisters. She told me he cried every day for years, and mom's younger sister, Dot slept with her, clinging to her, crying, and wetting the bed from despair each and every day.

When families tried to adopt my mother and she would be brought to their homes for trial, she would immediately act up so she could go back to the orphanage to be with her siblings. What must have been terribly painful for mom was that her mother went on to re-marry and have two more children that she raised - leaving her family of four in the orphanage up for adoption.

On mom's 16th birthday, she was given a suitcase for her clothes, $20.00, and was told it was time for her to leave and make her way in the world. She had to leave school and go to work in the city's mills making ice skates. Mom loved to ice skate, almost as much as she had loved school.

Dad and Mom got introduced and with their mutual love of skating — ended up spending time at Whalom Park's skating arena. My mother and her sister, Lorraine lived together when they left the orphanage. Mom was a mill worker by day, and skated away her free time either on the ice skates she made, or in the summertime on roller skates. Likewise, Dad made his livelihood in the paper mills, but used every free minute playing backyard sports. Eventually, Aunt Lorraine married Uncle Frank, another mill worker in the steam engine mill in Fitchburg. Mom and Dad married, and I was born less than two years

THE EARLY YEARS

a vegetarian from birth, so Sunday dinner at gram's was not a fun experience. It often ended with her or I in tears, but either way I knew I'd be grounded when we got home.

Dad understood how I felt about animals. When he and I went to see the cartoon Bambi, neither of us made it passed the opening scene when Bambi's mother was shot and killed by the hunter — we both left the theatre in tears. Mom never understood how we were so upset over a cartoon. Mom had learnt early on that you had to eat what you were given or go hungry; fortunately, I never had to master this lesson.

Mom stood slightly less than five feet tall, but she was a force to be reckoned with. Her strong will and my stubbornness would often clash. When she sent me to my room over my objection, I would climb the steep steps until there were three more steps to go and then I would stomp up the last three. Mom would fly up the stairs after me. "Get downstairs and walk up and down ten times," she would yell at me, and I would comply for 9 ½ flights — up and down — and then I would stomp again. This contest of personalities, or my defiance, could go on for hours. Then finally it would end. "Now, go to your room," said mom. At this point I would slam my door. The voice would penetrate upstairs, "Open and close your door ten times properly," and then we'd start over again. Mom would ultimately threaten, "Wait until your father gets home." I'd respond, "I'm shaking," and start to fake tremble all over. No one was afraid of Dad. If we deserved punishment, Mom better dole it out because dad didn't have it in him. We had Dad wrapped around our finger. We knew it. He knew it. And she knew it.

We lived three quarters atop a very steep hill. My parents purchased our home in 1957 for $8,000. My

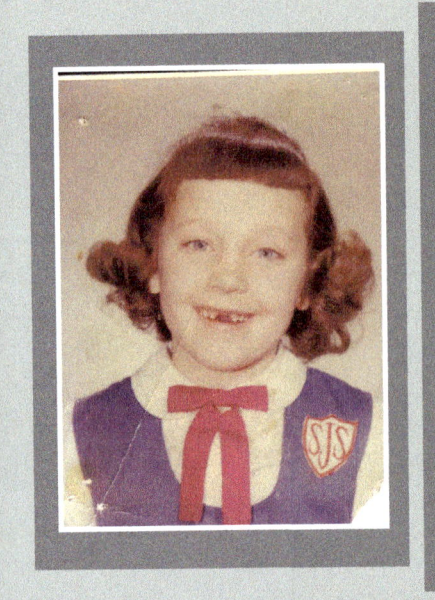

John and I

THE EARLY YEARS

grandfather loved to go to the horse races, something I morally oppose because of the inhumane treatment of the horses. If he were alive today, we'd fight about that. Gramps should have given up his driving long before he did, so whenever we rode in a car with him, you'd have to watch the curb to make sure he kept in the lane. Sometimes when I was young he would ask mom to drive him to the races. One night she kept his car, planning to bring it back the next morning because he had no night vision, so she didn't want him to drive. When mom parked the car in the driveway she failed to put the car in park. My second floor bedroom sat above the road. From my bed that evening, I heard some very faint cries, "Help, help, help"! I sprung up, and looked out. There was Grampy's car being held from the top of an embankment by MOM — 4'11", 104 pounds mom — to prevent the car from crashing into the neighbor's house!

I was a pretty outspoken kid - - so much so that by the time I reached the sixth grade the nuns and my parents mutually agreed that my loud, challenging voice would be better heard in public schools. When I joined the drama club and competitive plays, my voice was the only one that carried — loud and clear — to the last of the balcony. I remember that Martin Luther King, Jr. said, "Our lives begin to end the day we become silent about things that matter". No need to tell me to speak up. I was loud and had an opinion on everything.

I was in the first class that entered the new Junior High in town — called Memorial Junior High. I loved it there. We walked the one and one-half plus miles to school, even though my mother explained to the transportation department that in accordance with their own rules we were outside the distance that required walking to school. We were eligible for the bus. I remember when the

Life's Not Always a Day at the Beach

Superintendent picked her up to "go for a ride" to prove mom wrong. He had disbelieved our "old car" could accurately measure distance. She returned home grinning ear to ear because she was correct — so we could take the bus if we wanted. Mom usually won her battles.

Many years later, for two consecutive years, I was asked to be the graduation speaker at my Junior High School.

This is what I had to say:

> My Family is from Fitchburg. My father is one of the most Wonderful human beings on earth, but never had the opportunity to go to college. He worked all of his life in the paper mill in West Fitchburg, often 60+ hours a week in 100 degree temperature to provide for his family. My mother spent part of her life in an orphanage, and when she turned age 16 was forced to go to work and withdraw from high school. So, I was the first in my family to go to college and I did that the hard way. When I graduated from Fitchburg High School, I went to work as a teller in a local bank for $60.00 per week. When I saved enough money, I began attending college at night. The very first course I took --- and I only could afford one – was a business law course.
>
> I still remember thinking, somehow, some way, someday, I will get to law school. I worked my way up in the bank from teller, to head teller, to branch manager, and so forth, until I ultimately became Vice President of

THE EARLY YEARS

the medium sized commercial bank I then worked for. I went to law school at night and finally fulfilled my dream of being an attorney at age 35.

This is what I said about success.

To me, being successful isn't about money, or new BMW's or Rolex watches. It is about remaining true to the principles your family and teachers have instilled in you. It is about doing your best in all things. All the money in the world, cannot buy you character or respect.

I gave some specific tips for success:

1. Do not blame others for mistakes. Own up to them and move on;

2. Work hard to get a good education. Strive not to miss any days of school and to do your best work;

3. Be kind to others. The "nerds" are likely one day to be your bosses and the elderly, the mentally retarded, and the disabled need your help. Don't be cruel or you'll ultimately regret it;

4. Get involved. In sports, the class plays, the band, and so forth, but whatever you do, do it with passion;

5. Respect your elders;

6. Have a positive winning attitude, because it's your attitude that determines your success.

7. You should also keep yourself free of drugs and abusing alcohol; and

8. When you fail, as we all do, get up and press on. Remember, even Michael Jordan missed over 12,000 shots.

MY YOUNGER SIBLINGS NANCY AND MICHAEL

My sister, one of my closest allies, loves to fight when the circumstances warrant it. Her stories are larger than life and she is so much smarter than she is willing to let others know. She was a great athlete in her day, captain of her basketball team. At five foot three inches, Nancy played on the team that won the state championship. But for all her ferocity, she has a heart of gold, taking in all strays, whether four legged or of the two legged kind. Her home is like a homeless shelter with more kids than beds, and little money to go around. When Nancy was born, I was 14 and nothing pleased me more than having a sister. I often gave her advice that she generally ignored which has not changed much through the years. We are as different as night and day, but inseparable friends.

I was 21 when my brother Mike was born. The doctors recommended mom have an abortion because she was 44 years old, and in poor health. She would not hear of it so she spent most of her pregnancy in the hospital. Mike was, and still is, a bundle of energy and a top athlete who held many local sports records as a young man. He was

Nancy and I

Mike and Me

Life's Not Always a Day at the Beach

the apple of my dad's eye. The two would play baseball for hours, and the only closer father/son relationship is the one Michael now has with his own kids. Like Mike, his youngest son, Aidan John would play ball 24/7 if you let him. At age 4, his sports acumen leads me to believe he will be the family's best athlete, and his older brother, Colin, the family's best scholar. Colin is more responsible at age 9 than I am at age 61. He makes sure I wear my seat belt, monitors where I leave things like my purse, and gives me instruction on technical matters. He is a brilliant child. At age 2, he was in a body cast because of a severe break and not until the day the cast was sawed off did I hear this child complain or cry.

These two siblings, Colin and Aidan, are as different as a pair can be. My brother instructed them one day while they were in the water that they may not go in deeper than their mouth — meaning their mouths must be above water. Accordingly, Colin would go in no deeper than his shoulders; Aidan would have the water level brushing his lip. Colin is concerned about my "big" dogs, Aidan wants to ride them.

Mike, like my sister Nancy, is a fighter. Our parents made each of us volunteer when we reached the age we could legally work. "Do something for others before yourself" was their motto. I was a candy striper at the local hospital, but Nancy and Mike both volunteered to help mentally retarded citizens like our brother, John.

One day Mike had a van filled with disabled workers and they were sweeping at a public park. A group of punks decided to make fun of and harass those disabled workers which was more than my brother would tolerate. Rumor has it he put the workers in the van and instructed them only to open the door for him or

THE EARLY YEARS

the police, and then like a madman, leveled these assailants. My two younger siblings are definitely ones you want on your side. I am so lucky they have my back.

Massachusetts School of Law

lex et veritas

To all who may read these letters Greetings

Hereby it is certified that upon the recommendation of the faculty, the Trustees of the Massachusetts School of Law at Andover have conferred on

Diane M. Sullivan

the degree of

Juris Doctor, Magna Cum Laude

in recognition of the satisfactory fulfillment of the requirements pertaining to this degree

Dated this _first_ day of June 1990

_____ Dean

_____ Chairman of the Board of Trustees

THE DREAM OF BECOMING A LAWYER

It doesn't matter where you are coming from, all that matters is where you are going.

Brian Tracy

The ad jumped off the page at me. Commonwealth School of Law, Lowell, Massachusetts – part time programs. Applications being accepted for fall . . . Oh no, I still had four more college courses to take. Could I possibly take these courses in the summer sessions and be ready for law school in August? Law school had only been a dream – would this be possible? I made the call.

When the law school's catalog arrived, an impressive stone building with clock and turrets was on the cover. How exciting it would be to attend classes in such a prestigious looking place. I was hooked. Law school was no longer a fantasy for this mill worker's daughter. I could make it my reality.

Life's Not Always a Day at the Beach

On registration day, I headed to Lowell. How ironic was it that Lowell is one of the oldest mill cities in the United States? As I drove up and down the street, I was totally perplexed because I could not find the building displayed on the cover. In fact, I was in a blighted section of town. I pulled into a service station for help, calling to the attendant behind the glass, "Where do I find this law school", while simultaneously pointing to the picture on the cover of the catalog. The attendant shouted back, "that's city hall". "That law school is across the street." He pointed to a small, low, white professional, pretty utilitarian looking office building. It was too late to turn back now. I drove across the street, parked the car, and entered the building. Inside I learned that the building also housed professional offices including a chiropractic office. The chiropractor owned the building.

As much as I detested the building, I liked the other students I met. They were so excited to be there. Excitement turned to fear, however, when I looked at the books we needed to purchase. When I left the bookstore after registration day, I headed to my parents house to visit my mother. She would know what I needed to hear.

I told my mother of my fears. "Mom, my entire car is filled with books. I don't know if I can do this and work full-time. I am worried my dreams have exceeded my capabilities this time". "Withdraw," she said flatly. "You don't need this. You have been going to school at night for years, almost decades. What you need is a husband and family". I told her I could not turn back. I had already told everyone I was going to law school, including, the chairman of the bank I was employed at as Vice President. I already paid my tuition. I had to stay. My law school journey began. There was no way back.

THE DREAM OF BECOMING A LAWYER

From the first class on, I loved it but I was scared to death of failing. My favorite subject was contracts despite the intensity of the professor who tried to imitate the professor in the Paper Chase. During the very first class he took the roster and called the first name on it and asked her to stand up – Rosalie Bailee. He then proceeded to dissect Ms. Bailee. I thought to myself, this was cruel and totally unnecessary, and thank God my last name begins with an 'S'.

After a few weeks of classes, if you asked my 65 classmates who they thought was the least likely to make it, I would have won the vote. I was simply a mess trying to juggle it all: my running shoes were hanging from a light in my car, which was littered with food, clothes, and books. I had no idea what the course on civil procedure was about, and I was just struggling to keep up with reading and briefing my cases. It was the fourth week of classes that nearly put me in my grave. Our first legal writing and research project was assigned so I made my way to the school's law library, surrounded by aisles of books and no idea what to do. I felt my knees go weak. That evening as I headed for home I kept thinking about that assignment until I felt a tightening in my chest. I had been a runner for many years so I quickly dismissed the idea I was having a heart attack, but the pain worsened. Instead of turning off at my exit, I headed up the hill to the hospital. When I arrived at the entrance to the hospital ER the pains had dissipated. Was I, or was I not having a heart attack? No, probably not. I turned the car around and headed home.

The following week when I returned to the law library, many of my classmates were there working on the assignment. They seemed cool and in control so I told them about my "almost" heart attack, asking how they

Life's Not Always a Day at the Beach

were holding it together. One of my fellow classmates then piped up, "at least you didn't go into the hospital, I went by ambulance with chest pains".

As the semester progressed, I found myself settling down, but still my classmates would not have bet on my surviving. It all changed one Saturday afternoon in contracts class. The topic was contract consideration, and the professor went around the classroom, up and down the aisle, asking what the consideration was to support the contact. Students were nearly jumping out of their seats, standing, offering their input on what they believed was the consideration. The professor skipped over me until the end when he announced, "Ms. Sullivan please tell the class what the consideration is to support the contract. "There isn't any," I responded. "That's correct," he responded. No longer was I seen as the blind man lost in the forest. My classmates looked at me with a bit more respect. I could do this.

We formed a study group and we would often meet to review hypotheticals the professors provided, discuss cases, or simply offer each other a shoulder to cry on. The study of law becomes an all-consuming experience and unless you are engaged in it, it becomes hard to relate. Law students need each other.

I really never figured out what civil procedure was until the end of the semester, but somehow, while drawing up my course outline, I figured out the essence of it. I took my final exams and hoped for the best. I knew I had done the best I could, while wishing I didn't have a full-time job so I could have studied every waking moment. As it was, on Friday nights I rarely went to bed because I was preparing for a full day of Saturday classes.

We all assembled one Saturday in January in the

Law School

Early site of
The Massachusetts School of Law

THE DREAM OF BECOMING A LAWYER

school's administrative office to receive our first semester grades. When I approached the window, the president came running over to say, "I want to see her face when she opens the envelope". I did not know what to make of this. Trembling, I opened the envelope - - but by the luck of the Irish, and a lot of hard work, I had received nearly all A's. I thought: Wow, I really can do this. I will be an attorney.

At the time I enrolled in the Commonwealth School of Law, the school lacked degree granting authority, but I was led to believe it was a mere formality. Because of its low cost, it was a risk I was willing to take to achieve my dream. I thought it was my only shot at being an attorney. The price tag of the Boston law schools was out of reach. I hoped I was not so desperate and naïve to achieve my dream that I became a fool.

In December of 1987, after a law school inspection, the school's President, Michael Boland, indicated degree granting authority would be received quickly, so we enrolled for another semester with the few dollars most of us had left. When the inspection report came in, we found out the inspectors had found serious deficiencies with the school, including the need for a Dean. Many of us now knew, as classmate Dick Ahern had warned, that President Boland was not to be trusted. The law students pressured Boland to bring on a dean. Lawrence R. Velvel was then hired and brought on as dean. Velvel was tenacious with a resolve to never back down. He is a Michigan graduate, a Supreme Court litigator, a constitutional law professor, a scholar, and vocal Vietnam War opponent. He used his legal skills to challenge the war on constitutional grounds which were not popular with many people in the United States back then, and especially in the heartland of Kansas where he taught. Velvel later moved to Washington, D.C. as a professor at Catholic University, and then took a position in a major law firm, before arriving at Commonwealth School of Law.

In many ways, like us students, Velvel was duped by Boland. When Velvel first arrived we were relieved and optimistic about the future of the law school. We kept faith. Even if Boland would continuously test that faith.

The call came from my classmate and friend, Al Zappala, during my second year at Commonwealth School of Law. Zappala told me Boland was going to fire Dean Velvel. Zappala believed quite rightly that this would be bad news for the Board of Regents, perhaps the death knell for Commonwealth School of Law. We would never be attorneys. I fell silent. I saw my dream going up in smoke.

I asked to meet with Zappala at the school. He told me President Boland had bugged the school with secret recording devices. It was clear at this point the school would fail. The evidence was mounting that Boland was a criminal. It would get even worse. President Boland's firing of Dean Velvel was met with students screaming, classmates quitting, and many desperate law students making serious accusations of numerous improprieties. This was our "Black Saturday." Later that day, Zappala and Ahern called me to ask me to call Dean Velvel to ask him to help us start our own law school! Are they all crazy? What did we know about starting a law school? I barely knew Velvel. I had no faith that the three of us could help start and run a law school.

But over the next eight months we worked tirelessly to accomplish that goal. It's amazing what a committed group of people can do when they do not know any

THE DREAM OF BECOMING A LAWYER

better. On August 22, 1988, The Massachusetts School of Law in Andover opened its doors to ninety-four students - - fifty-four students transferring with us from the Commonwealth School of Law. Velvel was a founder and Dean, and was joined by Michael Coyne, who was, and is the heart and soul of MSL. Coyne had taught at Commonwealth as did his wife Jeanne. Coyne believed in the mission he helped establish because like so many students at the Massachusetts School of Law, he worked his way through college and law school – attending nights. Paula Kaldis also joined Velvel and Coyne as a founder and professor, and today is an Assistant Dean.

Velvel also brought on some of his classmates and friends from Michigan Law School, and his cousin, Joe Fishelson to MSL's Board of Trustees, and the Board of Regents were rightly impressed.

Commonwealth School of Law continued limping along, but the death knell had rung. Boland's criminal activity came to light, but even with those revelations, a number of prominent individuals joined Commonwealth's Board to try and salvage what to us was well beyond repair. It also became known that only one of the two law schools – Commonwealth or MSL would receive approval from the Commonwealth of Massachusetts and survive. Former United States Senator and Presidential candidate, Paul Tsongas aligned himself with Commonwealth School of Law. We hoped politics would not let evil triumph over good. We did not fear failure. MSL would succeed. We had no other option.

MSL was thriving, and I was in my last year of law school. Soon I would sit for the bar exam with MSL's anticipated approval by the Commonwealth of Massachusetts. As we approached the end of 1989, I was buried

Graduation from
The Massachusetts School of Law
June 1, 1990

THE DREAM OF BECOMING A LAWYER

in work at MSL's library. I looked around and only my classmate Juan Ortiz and I remained. It was nearly midnight. I knew I needed to head to my home an hour away, because I was due at work early the next morning. I decided to bring some books to my car. As I entered MSL's parking lot, I heard footsteps: Someone running away toward the back of the building. I ran back inside in search of Juan. I told him what I heard. I asked him to let me know when he was leaving, so we could walk together. Arriving home about an hour later, my phone was ringing - - there had been an explosion and fire at MSL.

One did not need to look far for suspects. Boland was previously suspected of arson for profit at his horse stables where a number of horses died. This time it was for hate and to destroy, or at least slow down, MSL's chance of success. When I later testified in Essex Superior Court at Boland's trial, I expressed my thanks that he at least waited until I left the building before attempting to blow it up.

Despite the significant efforts of others, MSL received degree granting authority in the Spring of 1990. On the first Friday of June, 1990, I and thirteen classmates graduated with a Juris Doctorate degree from the Massachusetts School of Law. MSL Trustee, Judge Isaac Bornstein opened the ceremony by proclaiming, "How sweet it is". As valedictorian, my remarks followed Judge Bornstein. Despite everyone telling us we could not do it, our "fantasy" became reality. No one should ever tell us that we cannot achieve our dreams.

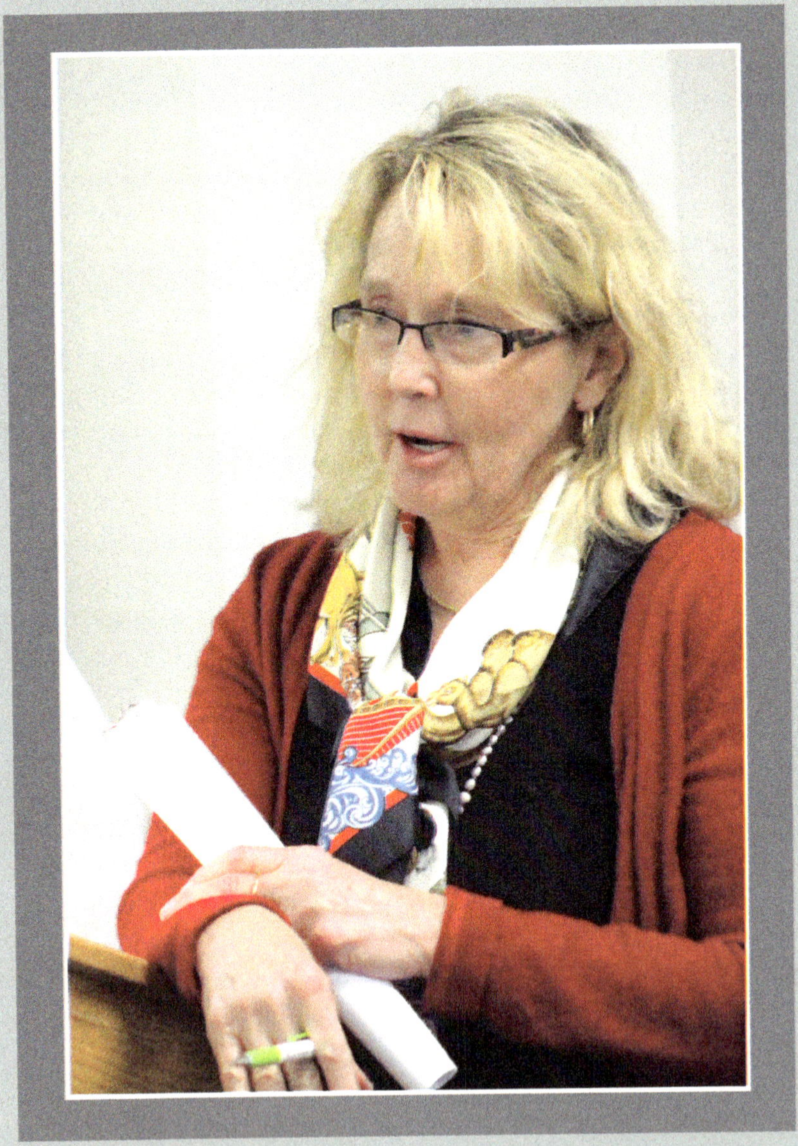

TRANSITION FROM STUDENT TO PROFESSOR

Let us rise up and be thankful for if we didn't learn a lot today, at least we learned a little, and if we didn't learn a little, at least we didn't get sick, and if we got sick, at least we didn't die. So let us all be thankful.
                                                Buddha

In retrospect, I wanted to be an attorney since I stood knee high, but for many years it did not appear to be a viable option for me. As the daughter of a mill worker from the City of Fitchburg, I became the first in my family go to college. I had to do it the hard way - - at night, one course at a time, saving coins in a piggy bank. I still remember that when I had saved enough money to enroll for my first college course, I signed up for business law. I was thinking, somehow, someway, someday, I will get to law school. But, that was really a wide eyed dream, something I am known for - - big dreams. I was a bank teller then, making $60.00 a week. When I got

Life's Not Always a Day at the Beach

my first raise of $3.00 a week from the man in the pinstripped suit@ for my superior performance, I quickly realized I better find a way to get an education. I would be damned before I'd settle for annual raises of $3.00. I knew an education was crucial - - for myself and to be able to help the people I cared about. But was the law - the profession I dreamed of- open to this commoner? I wasn't sure. My first college class continued to ignite my fire for the law. The professor told us, "I am going to treat you like law students". While other students groaned, I was elated. Bring it on, I thought. On my final examination the professor wrote on my paper that I belonged in law school. Yeah, I thought to myself, easier said than done. I still had to take 39 more classes to get my undergraduate degree.

So, finally at age 35, because the Massachusetts School of Law had opened its doors to me, I fulfilled my dream (which really had seemed impossible) of becoming an attorney.

MSL was founded on the premise there should be fair opportunity for the common man and woman. The roots of the school involve the question of whether the law, as a profession, will be open to the intelligent commoner of diligent application or will instead be open to what Hamilton called the rich, the wise and the well born. The school's philosophy is, and has always been, to provide opportunity for rigorous legal education and training to the less privileged person who has the intelligence, diligence and desire to make effective use of this opportunity.

To service its clientele of the less affluent persons, the school was economically affordable to me as it charged half of the tuition charged by many of Boston's other law schools. Because students at MSL generally (but not

Massachusetts School of Law
500 Federal St., Andover, MA

MSL Faculty at graduation
June 2, 2000

Life's Not Always a Day at the Beach

exclusively) work for small firms, for state governmental agencies, and even in solo practices, MSL teaches its students the professional skills needed to practice - - not just theoretical principles. MSL has been a pioneer in teaching essential professional skills with numerous courses in trying cases from the time the client walks into the office to the end of trial. All these courses are taught by full- time faculty who are not just professors but also are skilled practitioners, or by expert judges and lawyers.

MSL knew if it was to serve the common man - - if it is to serve the working class, the minority person, the woman in mid-life, the immigrant - - it must, and does follow an admission standard that allows capable, diligent persons admission. It cannot, like other law schools, do admission "by numbers". So MSL did not and does not use the LSAT (Law School Admission Test). All of this made law school accessible to me.

So, MSL, my school, begun 25 years ago and today has approximately 3,500 graduates. I was in the first graduating class and spoke at the school's first graduation. I asked the audience whether they had ever wanted anything so bad they could taste it? How fortunate I could realize my dream. Many people are not so lucky.

When Paula Kaldis called me to inquire whether I wanted to teach legal writing at MSL's writing program, I had to tell her "No". As much as I wanted to accept her invitation to join the faculty, I knew teaching writing was not a good fit for me. So reluctantly I declined.

A few months later, Peter Malaguti inquired into my interest in teaching. He said, he thought I would greatly miss the pursuit of academia. I knew he was correct. I was already missing it. So when the next call

Paula Kaldis, Esq.
Professor of Law

Michael L. Coyne, Esq.
Professor of Law

Peter M. Malaguti, Esq.
Professor of Law

Life's Not Always a Day at the Beach

came from my alma mater I jumped at the chance to teach secured transactions. Shortly thereafter, one of the contracts professors left MSL so I got asked to teach my favorite class - - contracts.

Since I had been a student of both Mike Coyne and Peter Malaguti and thought they were simply outstanding teachers, I tried to use their teaching style as a model, knowing I would never be quite as good as they are. I believe in hard work and feel a second-to-none work ethic is the key ingredient to passing the bar exam. I often think of a poster I once saw of a man sitting on top of a mountain that quoted Vince Lombardi, "The man on the top of the mountain didn't fall there." So any hope of passing the bar examination short of hard work I see as fool's gold. As a professor, I think it is important to make students work hard by demanding effort and preparation. These are the traits I strive to instill in our students.

In our law school it is easy to demand this type of effort because students at MSL are working for a better tomorrow. Their education at MSL will open a window of opportunity for them and their families, so, they are willing to work for this opportunity to better their life. Their agenda is bigger than themselves.

I teach students who have grown up in single family homes with mothers who work two shifts. In one small class, I had two young women who both lost teenage brothers to death by bullets in the city streets. These students have raised themselves and have somehow made it to law school. How different their lives will be because they have been provided this opportunity.

Because lawyers are engaging in a profession that requires adherence to rules, I have class rules with which that I require compliance. The first few weeks of the semester are often a tug of war - - them against me, but I know the outcome in advance. I will win. As I see it though, they win also.

Ultimately, as a lawyer in court you don't wear a hat so I don't allow hats in class. The guys, the jocks, really hate taking off their baseball cap. As much as I love the Red Sox, those caps are coming off. My biggest challenge though, came from Jill.

At the start of class, I told her she needed to remove her hat. Jill, who I liked a lot, despite the fact she was sassy, responded: "Professor, it is not a hat." "Really Jill", I said, "then what is that on top of your head? Enlighten the class", I said. Jill looked me squarely in the eye and says, "It is an 'accessory'". "Jill, if it quacks, it's a duck. If it's on your head with a feather coming out of the top, it's a hat. Remove it now"! She did. Everyone smiled and we got down to the class material. Later that day, I received a telephone call. It was Jill. She had dinner with her mother that evening. When Jill arrived at the restaurant her mom made her remove her hat. Jill thought we were in collusion, but we had a good laugh because she intended to complain to her mother about me, but before she had the opportunity, saw it would not work to her advantage.

Early in the semester I called on John, an older man, to brief a case. It is important that students learn how to identify the issue in the case. I asked John what the issue was. He looked at me blankly. I repeated the question. Still no response. I decided to help him out – "John," I said, "the issue is on page 138." No response. "John read the issue on page 138," I said. He now speaks for the first time, "I can't," he says. "John," I said, "of

Life's Not Always a Day at the Beach

course you can. Just open up your book and read it. I am not asking you to phrase it – the court does it for you. Just read it. Second paragraph, first sentence." No response. I was exasperated. I wanted to scream. "John open up your book to page 138. Open it and read the sentence." "I can't" he says again. Oh my God, I thought. "For the last time," I say "read the issue!" I am standing in the aisle now right aside of him with sixty students awaiting my next move. He says, "I'm blind Professor." If the earth would have opened up and swallowed me, I would have been grateful. We did press on though, and John finished the semester with the aid of some special equipment. He is a successful lawyer today.

It was about five minutes before my first Secured Transactions class when I entered the classroom and placed my book on the podium. As I looked out on the class, I saw many anxious faces, and among them was a young man, leaning back in his chair and eating his lunch from a number of tupperware containers. Cool as a cucumber. I said "Todd, do you intend to take your lunch with you to court also, or will you eat first". "Just finishing", he responded. I looked down now to discover, he also had his shoes off. So I thought, I'd better ask if he intended to wear shoes in court. He smiled, put on his shoes and it was time to start. I remember thinking, "this is going to be one long semester".

But what I quickly found out was this young man was one of the hardest working, brightest, most dedicated, respectful young man I have ever had the pleasure of teaching. He graduated at the top of his class.

In the same class was Dr. Joe. Doctor of what???? Podiatry. This explains why he always asked about my running and his odd obsession with my feet. So, why was

TRANSITION FROM STUDENT TO PROFESSOR

he in law school? Joe said in his application that after 15 years of running his own podiatry practice in Manhattan, he felt intellectually unchallenged and sold his practice. Boy, he should have had me as a patient.

What did Joe do next? You'll never guess!! He worked as a professional comedian. You know I should have figured this out because every time I saw Joe, he had a joke for me. Personally, I thought he was telling me to "lighten up". Joe performed live on national television several times and had a top 50 single hit.

If you ask Joe why law school, he'd tell you that nice Jewish boys became doctors not cops and he's now too old to be a cop. However, he is still seeking a law enforcement career. Joe intended to combine his background in the medical sciences with the study of law to focus on forensics and bio-technology. He is extraordinarily bright and hardworking and has the courage to follow his dreams, like thousands of the students that followed him.

Because I am very serious, most people don't expect a practical joke from me. So my April Fool's jokes generally work out pretty well. When I was a kid I often ended in big trouble on April Fool's Day. The only question on April 2nd was how long I had been grounded for – a day, a week, or two. The joke I pulled on my contracts class was no exception. I entered the classroom at the scheduled time, 2:30 p.m.

With a stack of bluebooks that are used for examination purposes, I told the students to clear their desks and put all their personal items against the walls of the classroom. You could actually see their looks of horror. They were petrified. I had them in the position I wanted. I passed out the bluebooks telling them they had the class

Life's Not Always a Day at the Beach

period to complete the exam which would represent 20% of their final grade. All of the students believed me. When I told them to open their bluebooks and begin, this is what they saw:

APRIL FOOLS!!

TRANSITION FROM STUDENT TO PROFESSOR

One October I saw the sign, source unknown, to dress up for Halloween; I thought that would be fun. So did my colleague and dear friend, Professor Rudnick who came to MSL dressed as a witch. Before I went to work that Halloween morning, I dug in my basement for items from which to make a costume. I decided a hobo would work. I grabbed some old jeans, complete with tar from paving the driveway. I had a plaid shirt, some old work boots and a mask with a wig attached. I went to the woods to get a walking stick and tied a bandanna on it. After I got dressed and looked in the mirror, I was quite pleased with my appearance - - I was unrecognizable, at least at first blush, I thought.

When I headed upstairs to the classroom to teach my law class, I decided to take a seat, as though I was a student. The class start time was 2:30 p.m., and I always require prompt attendance so all the students were there by 2:25 p.m.

When I took my seat among the class it was apparent they did not know it was me. When the clock hit the 2:30 mark, I stayed seated unsure of what my next move would be, as I had not planned on not being recognized for this long a period. So, it should not have surprised me when the class started to talk about me, and they did. And I didn't know what to do. "So, where is she? Ms. Never can you be late!!!" They were ranting about me ..... mocking me, actually. Finally, I couldn't fake it anymore so I stood up and went to the podium. The students gasped in horror as I took off the mask and started to teach. Boy, did the prank back-fire!

I have lunch with my brother, John every Wednesday and Saturday. I went that same Halloween day to pick John up in my costume, and like my students John

Yep, that's me with the Nobile kids!

TRANSITION FROM STUDENT TO PROFESSOR

didn't recognize me. I kept signaling to him to come, but he stood shaking his head "No;" he was afraid. When he discovered it was me, he laughed harder than ever. Now each year, John expects me to dress up before our Halloween visit.

At the beginning of each semester I have students make signs with their name on it so that I am free to move around the room and call on students by seeing their name displayed on the sign. Usually, after a month or so I know most of the students by name. There was one student I could never keep straight. I'd call him Tom, he would hold up his sign saying I'm Steve. I'd make a mental note, and it would seem when I call him Steve, he'd hold up his sign saying, Tom, etc. He was very professional in his appearance, owned a real estate office. Never did I figure out he had signs with different names on each side.

Then there was Nealy. I met her when she was a student in my contracts class.

It was the second day of class when I saw the back door of my classroom open and someone exit. I did something then that I had never done or did again - - I left the podium, exited the door in the front of the classroom and chased down the student. "Where do you think you're going?" I yelled . . . The student turned - - the most beautiful young woman I had ever seen, looked me in the eyes, totally cool and said – "I have somewhere I have to go" - - "Not during my class you don't – get back there and don't ever do this again". I thought - this one is trouble. She's smart – beautiful, and has chutzpah.

What I did not realize then was that this young woman would become my colleague and very dear friend.

Life's Not Always a Day at the Beach

Nealy's family, the Daryabegi family, an Iranian family are the kindest, smartest, are amongst the most generous family I have ever known. They are truly a beautiful and special family. I love them dearly. One day, Nealy was wearing a beautiful gem and I told her how beautiful it was. She then wanted to give it to me. It was always the same story. I never told her how much I loved her car because I was afraid a Lexus would arrive in my driveway.

After Nealy graduated from law school, passing the bar exam the first time, she was hired by the Massachusetts School of Law. She was a faculty favorite. We adored Nealy because of her spunk, humor, intelligence, generosity, kindness, and love of kids and family.

Nealy contributed in the early years to the law school's weekly television show, making the TV productions into a national award winning program. She did it all – wrote scripts, found guests, did production, on-air interviews, and arranged for national distribution. Because of her efforts, we received some of the most prestigious awards in the industry. She was a perfectionist - - striving to make us look good. She told me one day –"don't wear a turtleneck on the air again – put on your TV- do you see people wearing turtlenecks? No because it makes everyone look too heavy. And don't be telling people you don't watch TV – they'll think you're weirder that you are". Guess what? I never wore a turtleneck again. In fact, I went home and gave them all away!

Through the years – Nealy was a trusted confidante. I cannot tell you how much I missed seeing her everyday after she moved to California, but we would chat on the phone, and those calls were some of the happiest times for me. I'd end up sobbing with laughter from her

Nealy Daryabegi

Life's Not Always a Day at the Beach

tremendous wit.

Nealy knew of the serious illness I now face. She was more concerned about me than herself. She told me, "I'll be coming out soon to take care of you - - I just need to get a little bit stronger - my mother and father are coming so I am going to come and take care of you for a few months." I had seen Nealy in June and knew how sick she was. So, I started to laugh – you are going to take care of me? I laughed uncontrollably. She said: "funny, Yasmin (her sister) laughed as hard as you when I told her my plan." I said "Nealy, I'm o.k." Nealy asked, "Who is going to take care of you"? "Who will get you a cold drink from the fridge when you need it? "I want to know what WOMAN WILL TAKE CARE OF YOU – I AM COMING."

I received a call on December 23rd that Nealy was in a coma. Yasmin kept me updated through Nealy's final days. Christmas was over, so I began undecorating my house. I went into the basement to get a box to put away some decorations. I found an old, big box – but inside the box were some broken bulbs from a previous Christmas. As I dumped out the pieces, a card also fell out - - the card was years old – it was from Nealy wishing me happiness. I received the dreaded message of Nealy's passing just 20 minutes later. Even in the end, Nealy takes care of her friends!

The MSL community is a family - - we are more like siblings than colleagues. Because MSL was founded to provide opportunity to those typically frozen out of law school, people like me, all of the faculty have signed on and believe in this mission. When asked by our board whether we ever desired to become a more traditional law school, the collective answer was a resounding NO! The support staff, secretarial, administrative, are as talented

TRANSITION FROM STUDENT TO PROFESSOR

as the faculty - - and are indispensable to the school's success. The school's full-time faculty is small and mighty, but enhanced greatly by our adjunct faculty comprised of judges and seasoned lawyers.

Having said all that though, if you were to ever join us for lunch, you'd leave bewildered, best case scenario. We are lawyers with an opinion on everything, and even when we don't know the facts, we express it even if just to generate controversy.

From time to time we fight with each other, and even play pranks on each other, but in the end we care for each other like a close family member. Once in a while we discuss our school as a television series deciding which actor/actress would play each faculty member. We have thought the Dean most resembles Malcolm McDowell, or Ed Asner in his character Lou Grant. I like Sean Connory, or Liam Neeson to play Mike Coyne. We all feel Danny DeVito or Dennis Farina is Tony Copani. Hugh Laurie for Professor Joe Devlin; Joe Pesci for Professor Philip Coppola; Vin Diesel for I.T. Director, Dan Harayda; Cindy Crawford for Lynn Bowab; Sandra Bullock could be Kathy Perry in financial aid, and the late Suzanne Pleshette as Connie Rudnick.

One of my favorite memories is known as "The Muffin Memo", from decades ago, a story to this day that has never been told. When our new Library Director was hired, we all received a memo from our Dean not to eat or drink in the library. The next morning, Professor Connie Rudnick snuck in her muffin in a bag and sat eating it sheepishly in front of her office in the library. My colleagues decided it would be funny to send her a mock memo from the Dean, the essence of which scolded her for "disobeying his orders". I was sworn to secrecy, but knew

Life's Not Always a Day at the Beach

Connie would "flip out" when she retrieved this memo from her box. I decided to come in late that day, once this "joke" was over, but first I told another staff person not to let it go far.

Well, the memo was left in her box; Connie reacted as I thought she would – yelling "over a muffin"!!! My colleagues knew they went too far, and stood in horror as Connie reacted, but when they told her it was a joke (because she never finished the memo, which disclosed it was a joke) everyone had a good laugh, especially Connie.

Connie Rudnick, Esq.
Professor of Law

Larry and I on set of an early
MSL Educational Forum

Band of Sisters guests:
Gunny Sergeant Rosie Noel,
Captain Vernice Armour,
Author Kirsten Holmstedt

MSL'S TELEVISION SHOWS

Television could perform a great service in mass education, but there's no indication its sponsors have anything like this on their minds.
                                        Tallulah Bankhead

      I will never forget the day the Dean, Larry Velvel, called me to his office and told me that academia has always been criticized for its failure to bring important information to the man and woman on the streets of the community in which the institution sits. Thus, feeling the criticism to be rightly deserved, he decided that the Massachusetts School of Law should produce public awareness programming on important topics that the mass media doesn't sufficiently cover. "I would like you to do this," he said. Me? I was the one person on the faculty who hadn't owned a television for over 20 years! If I had wanted to produce television programming I

Life's Not Always a Day at the Beach

would have gone to Emerson College and not law school. This was absurd. I then convinced myself that the Dean would forget this crazy idea, not that he was one to ever forget anything. I decided to just ignore him and hope this project, and his moment of temporary insanity, would go away - - permanently.

A few days passed and he said nothing about television shows. I felt relieved. I know the project was beyond my capabilities, so best he forgets it. We started a law school, wasn't that enough? Or did we really need to become a television production house?

Five days had passed since the Dean mentioned his idea for a television series to me. Then he stopped me to ask how the television show was coming along. Oh my God. Larry is serious about this, and I am going to have to do it.

So, where does one begin? Call the networks. The fact that I was calling on behalf of the law school at least got my calls past the receptionist. I surmised the networks took my calls because they were afraid I was suing them. When the major and ultimately minor networks heard why I was calling - - to ask to let the law school use their studio to produce a talking head show on important topics – the answer was generally the same – it will cost a lot of money.

A small non-profit law school that strives to keep costs down so that it is affordable to persons who have typically been frozen out of law school does not have "lots of money" to spend on public service. As always, I turned to Mike Coyne for guidance, and his smart advice. He suggested I talk with a local cable guy, Barrett Lester, who headed a little local cable facility in the neighboring

MSL'S TELEVISION SHOWS

City of Lawrence.

Figuring I was almost out of options I met with Barrett, and much to my surprise, Barrett was not only receptive to the idea, but was enthusiastic and the only beacon of hope for this project. In hindsight, it was an easy assignment for him and his very talented crew. Each show would be on a different topic of great importance with a panel of experts. The job of the program host was similar to a law professor.

Our first program aired in January of 1996, airing initially in fourteen local communities on Continental Cablevision. Today our programs air throughout new England on Saturday afternoons on the New England Cable News channel (NECN), and Sunday mornings on the Comcast Sports Network, as well as various other stations throughout the country. Our programs explore important topics with depth, as opposed to sound bites.

I've been arrested, handcuffed, thrown in a cell and prosecuted - - much to the delight of my students and television audience. The shows explored the inner workings of the judicial system.

We hope that our shows reflect the great works that our profession is capable of. We believe that with an informed citizenry, we have a better chance of the public recognizing the greatness that the legal profession is capable of and how hard our judges, district attorneys, defense attorneys, police officers, clerks, court officers, litigators and others work on a daily basis to insure our justice system is in fact a just one.

Thus, we are deeply committed to providing education, opportunity and information to all, and dedicated to

Dan Rea from WBZ, Judge Nancy Gertner,
Me and Attorney Victor Garo at MSL Law Day

One of Our Gracie Awards

MSL'S TELEVISION SHOWS

making a difference and understanding about what we do as lawyers.

Our shows have won a total of 437 awards, including Gracie Allen Awards for best TV talk shows. Last year our Massachusetts School of Law (MSL) Educational Forum program was nominated for a 35th Boston/New England Emmy Award. "In Defense of Women" was one of seven finalists being considered in the interview/discussion category, which recognizes excellence in a program, series or special consisting of interview/discussion material that is at least 75% unscripted.

Kathryn Villare serves as producer/director/editor on the program, and Pamela Coffman did the camera work. I was lucky enough to host the show.

In her book, Judge Nancy Gertner writes about her struggle to succeed personally and professionally in a "stubbornly male profession." Defending clients in some of the most prominent criminal and civil rights cases of the time, Gertner drove home the point that women lawyers belonged in our courtrooms.

The awards were presented on Saturday, June 2, 2012, in a ceremony at the Marriott Boston Copley Place. We did not win. Hopefully we will get to the stage another year!

Let me take you on a few of our television trips.

Kathy and I at the
2012 GRACIE AWARDS LUNCHEON
Beverly Wilshire Hotel
Los Angeles, CA

TV TRIPS WORTH MENTIONING

TRIP TO HOLLYWOOD

I was thrilled when we received notice of receiving a Gracie Allen Award for best television talk show in the country. It really is a significant achievement for us. The award ceremony was in Los Angeles and all the female stars would be there.

As happy as I was that we had won this prestigious award, I was more excited about going to L.A. to receive it because it would provide an opportunity for me to stop in and see Nealy, who was living in Laguna Beach.

I booked the flights, but my traveling companion made the car rental reservation and hotel reservation. The thought was that we would fly out after work Friday, and with the three hour time change, arrive in L.A. by

Life's Not Always a Day at the Beach

9:00 p.m., and stay somewhere between the airport and Nealy's home. The next morning we would proceed onto Nealy's.

On our departure day we left and arrived in L.A. without a hitch. What I did not know was our car rental company was some deep discount – el cheapo – company. So, as we stood at the car rental shuttle pick-up area in the L.A. airport, it didn't take long to realize that no shuttle pick-up was coming. We waited . . . waited some more . . . made calls, and waited some more. I was tired and out of patience. Hertz drove by us, Enterprise, and several others kept circling around, but no el cheapo shuttle. It was midnight when we decided to flag down an Enterprise shuttle, even though we had no reservation. The shuttle driver was willing to take us to the Enterprise terminal, which we arrived at along with fifty other people, at about 1:00 a.m.

Obviously, Enterprise wasn't expecting this because they only had two windows open to service all the people waiting. After waiting in line for half an hour, and moving up only a few places, we got out of line and left the building knowing it would be dawn before we were serviced, and uncertain whether they would even have any cars left.

We convinced the shuttle driver for Enterprise to give us a lift as he headed back to the airport. We asked to be dropped off at a Dollar Rental, but he could only get us half a mile from the facility. So there I was at 2:00 a.m. California time (5:00 a.m. Eastern time) with all my luggage half a mile from where we needed to get to.

I strapped what I could on my back, but couldn't stand erect because of the weight of my baggage. I began taking baby steps toward the destination. When I finally arrived at Dollar Rental, I put down the luggage, and before you could blink I fell asleep atop my luggage. When my companion awoke me, we left the terminal with the rental car in search of the hotel. Do you think we could find our hotel? No. After an hour of driving around – up and down exit ramps – we ended up where we started. Oh my goodness. After threats of mayhem, we arrived at the hotel which was located nearby to the car rental facility - as the sun was breaking through the clouds: oh, what a night!

AND THEN THERE WAS THE FLORIDA TELEVISION SHOOT, AND IT WASN'T A VACATION!!

The book seemed to appear from nowhere among the pile of papers on my desk - - "Heroes For My Daughter" by Brad Meltzer. I remember thinking that I have no daughters, only nephews, but intrigued, I opened it.

> *Never give in. Never give in. Never, never, never - in nothing great or small, large or petty - never give in, except to convictions of honor and good sense....You have enemies? Good. That means you've stood for something, sometime in your life.*
>
> Winston Churchill.

Those same words are taped up on my office wall, except for the part about enemies. I had never heard that before. I was captivated. Stories, pictures and quotes from sixty inspirational people collected by the author. This book should be a television show, our next episode, I thought. Our Director apparently had the same thought, because she was the one who put the book on my desk.

View from our hotel.

TV TRIPS WORTH MENTIONING

I contacted the author, who lived in Florida to see if he would come up to do a television show. He quickly responded. No, sorry. Book tour is over, not coming to Massachusetts.

This was too bad, I thought. The book has great potential, and when I told this to Kathy I should have expected she would attempt to convince me to go there. Absolutely not, I said at first. Hauling enough equipment through security onto an airplane from Massachusetts was not my idea of a good time, besides the fact I am ill and the timing was not good for me. Emotion gave into logic and reason. I contacted the author to see if he would be receptive to doing a show if we came there. Sure, he responded. So, I told Kathy to schedule the taping at his house and we would fly down. A short time later, an exasperated Kathy told me he would not let us tape at his house because of his young children. So, that is it - show idea over.

But not accepting defeat, Kathy suggested we could tape outside somewhere. I decided to rent a studio in the area. Although that would have been a great remedy, it was too expensive for a law school producing programming for free as a public service. So, I gave in – collapsed under pressure and agreed to haul all the equipment for a two person interview on board a flight bound to Florida. We would leave Saturday afternoon, do an early Sunday morning shoot and come right back. "The best made plans of mice and [wo]men."

I decided to rent a room on the water in Ft. Lauderdale that we could use to shoot the interview. The first inkling of trouble came when the author's wife booked a surprise weekend vacation for his family. No real problem though, we could do the interview after and fly back

Life's Not Always a Day at the Beach

first thing Monday morning. I could be back to work for noon, or so I thought.

The Friday before we left, the hotel sent the confirmation of our stay and included the weather forecast for the weekend; 88 degrees and thunderstorms. For the first time ever, I decided to pack light - - usually I need a U-Haul to get my luggage curbside to airport. Not this time though! I went to have my hair done before we left - - one less thing to have to hassle over.

My nephew was playing on the United States National Ball Hockey Team for the bronze medal at the same time as our commute to the airport. Other than that, the flight from Logan to Ft. Lauderdale was uneventful. Deplaneing out the back door was a new experience, especially carrying baggage, cameras, and equipment down the portable stairs, and along a marked path on the runway. Being the first one off, I had no idea which way to go and was really concerned that the approaching plane would take me out. I saw a person up ahead dressed in an orange jacket, waiving at me frantically, so at that point I decided to stop walking which proved to be a good decision because I would have been flattened by an incoming plane.

I was hoping the rental car office was in the airport, but of course it wasn't. It was a short bus ride, but carrying the equipment made it seem like a journey of 100 miles. I kept my head down and leaned forward knowing that if Kathy had to stop one more time and wait for me she would rip the equipment from my arms telling me to eat my Wheaties. Really Kathy, I'm not a truck!

We got to the rental car finally, loaded up and were on our way to the hotel "suite" I had reserved. My definition of suite means more than one room. My definition was not synonymous with theirs, which consisted of just a room and a two-seat sofa. Even ignoring that, "on the water" could not reasonably have been construed to mean a side room without a water view.

I went to the front desk to protest and demanded the room I had reserved. It should have been a quick fix, except there was a huge swimming championship going on with most of the national swimmers (or so it appeared) staying at this hotel. After several attempts, we did get a better room, but never the "suite" I reserved. It proved nearly impossible to orchestrate because the elevators broke and it would take forever (slight exaggeration) to fight through the crowds with equipment to look at "rooms", but eventually I gave up and claimed the next room as ours.

The Director then wanted to scope out a location near the water to tape the "open and close" to the show. So we headed out to accomplish this before dark. At that precise moment the sky turned dark, a bolt of lightning appeared and it started to pour. So much for my hair I just had done. I tried to run back to the hotel, but the good Samaritan with me - - our show director – decided we needed to help some street musicians save their equipment and told me to help get the equipment under cover. So there I stood in the pouring rain, in my television clothes, and hair soaking wet - - no problem. I'll start over tomorrow when the sun comes out, I thought.

The morning was rainy at first, but when it stopped we headed out to do some taping. At the precise moment I was able to tape, the sky opened up and once again there we stood in the pouring rain again - - I suggested a covered canopy area in front of "Bubba Shrimp" Restaurant.

**Kathy and I hangin' out
at the Bubba Gump Shimp Co., FL
(sneakers and box of chocolates included!)**

TV TRIPS WORTH MENTIONING

You know, 'run Forest run - - Bubba Gump Shrimp Co'. We then made our third attempt, but the T.V. camera didn't work, so we then abandoned the taping and headed to our rooms to try to dry the camera with a hair dryer. In our room we turned on the weather channel – Tropical Storm Debbie – Hurricane Warning. On my God! A storm with a name, a prediction of one foot of rain and hurricane warnings – how am I going to get out of here?

Kathy began to work on converting a hotel room into a studio, while intermediately checking on the hair dryers drying out the camera. It was then she realized the headphones were missing so we knew we needed to retrace our steps with the slightest hope we would find them. Since we were the only fools outside in the near hurricane, we did actually retrieve our headphones and returned to the room to dry out my last pair of shoes and clothes.

Trying to convert the room to a studio was nearly impossible. To say the storm outside made the lighting nearly impossible is an understatement. Kathy wanted to start moving furniture from other rooms into the room, but I had to remind her that the security cameras would probably depict her as a thief, and going to jail was not in my plans for the day. Thankfully, she abandoned the idea.

We kept working - - pressing on with the notion we would walk to a frozen yogurt store nearby for lunch/dinner before the television shoot. I can be bought with frozen yogurt. It seemed only fitting when we arrived to find the owner locking the door. A sign on the door read: No Business, Hurricane – Closed Early.

The author was scheduled to arrive at 5:00 p.m. So,

when 5:15 p.m. came and went, Kathy went downstairs to await him. She saw a man outside in the storm trying to retrieve his credit card from the parking meter. Yes, he was here!

In the meantime – I checked every airline and option for a flight back. There was only one seat on one outbound flight to Boston, but the problem was it had a connection - - in Puerto Rico.

Well, the interview went great. We then reconverted the room back from a studio and packed to head for home praying our early morning departure would happen despite "the hurricane." When we arrived at the airport at 5:00 a.m. we saw our flight was scheduled to depart "On Time". I grabbed a quick breakfast, cracked my tooth, and headed for a rocky ride home!

On Feb. 21, 2013, we were notified that the Massachusetts School of Law Educational Forum won its 7th Gracie Allen Award for the show, "Heroes for My Daughter".

AND THEN THERE WAS: "THE WOMEN IN GOVERNMENT" SHOOT A/K/A THE WASHINGTON TRIP

We decided to do a show focusing on women in government. We featured Salem Mayor Kim Driscoll (an MSL graduate) and the first female Attorney General of Massachusetts, Martha Coakley. We also wanted at least one national figure, a senator or congresswoman. We tried to get Susan Collins or Olympia Snowe from Maine, but no deal. It was election season for Collins and she would not make the time. So we finally reached Eleanor Holmes Norton from the District of Columbia. Terrific, except we

MSL Ed Forum: Women In Government
Congresswoman Katherine Clark,
Mayor Kim Driscoll,
Attorney General Martha Coakley,
Host Connie Rudnick,
and
Author Dr. Caroline Heldman

Life's Not Always a Day at the Beach

would now have to travel to D.C. to do the shoot. We set the date, Kathy, George on camera, and I would go down.

On the day we were to travel, for reasons I cannot recall, George had to bail out and left just the two of us to drag the equipment around Washington D.C. I drove to Manchester, NH airport for our Southwest flight to Baltimore. I dropped Kathy off at the door with all the equipment, and then went to park the car. We then waited for the flight. Kathy was wondering how on earth we were going to drag the equipment around Washington D.C. When we got to Baltimore, all our bags came too, which was a promising start. We rolled them out to the curb and onto the rental car bus, then off the bus, and into the rental car office. We needed an SUV and a couple of strong men, but Kathy and I loaded the rental with the equipment. Kathy drove and I climbed into the passenger seat. Kathy put the address in the GPS, and off we went. In a matter of minutes (after taking motion sickness pills), I was out cold, so Kathy drove in silence with the GPS guiding her in the darkness to the hotel. "Wake up Di, we are here" Kathy said. I was beginning to like this trip. We checked into the hotel, set the alarm for a few hours later, and got up the next morning to the hotel continental breakfast. It was quickly time to pack and check out. Now, who was it that said television is glamorous? We headed off to the senate building and thanks to the GPS, we found the building. But one major problem surfaced. Congresswoman Norton's office did not arrange for parking. So around the block we go, and go and go. Finally we give up. I get out with the equipment and sweet-talk the guard into helping me get inside, and through security. Meanwhile, Kathy drives around and around and around looking for parking. I drag the equipment to Representative Norton's office, no easy task, and unpack what I could. The Congresswoman's Aid tells me that Congresswoman

The U.S. Capital Building
Congresswoman Eleanor Holmes Norton

Life's Not Always a Day at the Beach

Norton has a busy schedule and we need to get this done on time (in 15 minutes). Fifteen minutes! I know I will be lucky if Kathy's back in an hour. I panic, call Kathy who was blocks away, walking to the building. Finally, after navigating Kathy to the office, she arrived hot and perspiring from the walk, and in a total panic.

Eleanor arrived and then said she had plenty of time so whenever we are ready is fine with her. We did the interview, which went well, repacked all the equipment, and began the long walk back to the car. Of course the wheel broke on the big suitcase, so we drag it the rest of the way to the car with Kathy yelling to me trailing behind, "You need to eat Wheaties". Hey, I thought I was the "talent"? And talent doesn't normally haul the equipment.

Next, we need to shoot the open and close. Once again, where to park? After a few drives around the mall and outlying areas, we finally find a spot. So once again we pull out the equipment, and walk to the mall in downtown Washington so we can have the White House behind us. One major problem now: NO FOOD! We were fading - - more precisely ready to hit the pavement. We were so busy we did not have time to eat and most places were not open. We give up and get back into the car, look at the time and decide we need to head to the airport with a box of popcorn from a street vendor. And wouldn't you know, TRAFFIC! Not just a little, the highway is STOPPED. Once again, panic; will we make it back to the airport in time? So driving from D.C. to Baltimore we go. Go, Stop, Go, Stop, Stop, Stop, all the way to Baltimore, the GPS telling us the traffic is stopped, but that this is the best route. IT DOES NOT HELP THE SITUATION! Finally, we get to the rental car return, not one minute too soon. The turn line is long and I can't wait. I asked if we can

TV TRIPS WORTH MENTIONING

just leave the car because we were running late. The car rental place says "yes" and I took off running. We drag the equipment to the rental bus and off we go to the airport, hoping to make it on time. Finally, we're at the airport. We drag the suitcases into the airport, check them in and head to security. Now we're at the gate, waiting to board, exhausted, and hungry and wanting to get home. We board and back home we go......The shoot was a success and the show won a Gracie Allen Award. But then the rental car company called me to say they are reporting to security that we stole the car ... Really.

THE NEW YORK TRIP

I received an email from a lawyer in town, Lois Karfunkel which read:

Subject: Women in America
I thought you might be interested in reading the excerpt below from Gail Collins' new book. Ms. Collins is a columnist for The NY Times, and she describes in her book, life as women knew it some 50 years ago, and continuing today. Her stories surely ring true for me, and perhaps you. Lois

This email intrigued me because I am always thinking about what women's shows can we do. I read the article in Time Magazine about the book, "What Women Want; Then & Now," and looked at some of the accompanying research Time Magazine provided.

Because I was still interested, I got the book and began reading it. Yes, this would make a great television show, and Gracie Award entry.... I contacted Gail, which began a series of back and forth phone calls and emails,

Life's Not Always a Day at the Beach

to set up the interview. No, she would not come to Boston, but we could go to her office in Manhattan. Next, she asked me to cut down the questions, there are too many. Oh my God. Boy, this is going to be a tough interview, I thought. A date was set, the outline worked on, intros and closes are written and put on large white poster boards to be read in Times Square (we hoped). Reservations were made at the Hampton Inn in Manhattan, a van was rented for the trip; all was set.

It is January 13, 2010, all the equipment is packed and in the van, and we begin to drive the 228.18 miles to New York in the snow, and Kathy, our producer, is as sick as can be. Kathy has a head cold that will not go away, so she is in the back seat while Pam drives - Talking all the way.... four hours plus. We arrive in Manhattan and find our hotel. It has one of those underground parking garages that has a very small elevator to the reception desk. So, one at a time, juggling equipment and tempers, we all take our turn in the elevator. The hotel rooms were nice, but we needed to eat. We drop everything in the room and decide to walk down the street for dinner. Pam has suggested a restaurant she and her husband ate at recently. So we went (later wishing we had gone to the Olive Garden we saw). The place was small and dark and too expensive for our budget but we ate there anyway. Kathy decided to see where the Times Building was, and then back to the hotel for a good night's rest, or as good as you get when you travel out of state hoping that all your equipment will work, and that you did not forget anything, and that the interview will go well.

Early in the morning we walked to Times Square from the hotel, which was not far, but with the wind kicking up it was very cold air. We reach our destination and set up for the shoot. Everyone passing by stared at us and

Times Square
Pam Sinton-Coffman and I

Life's Not Always a Day at the Beach

probably wondered if they should know me because I was doing all the talking into the camera. They surrounded me asking for an autograph. I responded, "You don't want my autograph, I'm no one famous". They persisted so I signed autographs while the police waited impatiently. Kathy made me stand on a barrier which triggered security. We shot our show's open but Kathy did not like the backdrop so we shifted to the other side that had all the playbills in large poster forms in the background. As soon as we shifted to the other side, a New York City police officer came over and asked what we were doing. I had to do a lovely little shuffle, explain what was up, that we would not be very long; so reluctantly, he let us continue. After a few takes, we shifted one more time for the close and packed up to head to the New York Times building. I complained so much about how cold it was, and the assistant producer joked on that Kathy was out of patience. What else was new?

We went quickly back to the hotel to pack up everything and drive over to the Times building. We found it with no problem, parked and unloaded. We were early, hoping to set up and be ready to go, but no dice. They would not even let us beyond the lobby until 1:00 p.m. Great! Next, came the bomb sniffing dogs to check us out. Finally we were allowed to go upstairs, but not in the main elevator. We had to go down around outside, through a separate door and into a freight elevator to get up to the office. We next traveled down a few corridors past some beautiful offices with great views of Time Square and Manhattan, and were excited to use the view as backdrop. But we ended up in a WHITE WALLED Conference room with NO WINDOWS, as boring a setting as possible. GREAT!

The interview (surprisingly) went extremely well,

and well over the time limit, which made us all wonder what her problem in the beginning was, and why she cut out the questions. We packed our bags and headed down the elevator. This time we used the main elevators as the intern who lead us did not know the back freight way. So, we did not mind that at all. We thanked everyone and headed back to the van for the trip home. Too many one way streets in Manhattan, too tall buildings for the GPS to work, so it took us a while to get out. We were famished as we had NO FOOD AGAIN.... thinking we would stop somewhere outside of the city. We were mistaken, THERE IS NO PLACE RIGHT OUTSIDE THE CITY. And naturally we hit traffic and more traffic. Pam pulled off the main road and headed down some back roads she knew because her father used to live in Connecticut. We finally found a diner and had some dinner. We arrived back at MSL late, unloaded, and all went home. Another glamorous television trip!

SO, WHAT'S A LITTLE CHEMO?

The cover of Time Magazine grabbed me: "What Ever Happened to Upward Mobility?". The author was Rana Fahrooha the assistant managing editor of Time. This is the heart and soul of our law school - - our mission. I really wanted to make this into a show so we started the back and forth emails and phone calls to set up the interview. The date was set for March 8, 2012. We once again would have to travel to New York. I rented a van and Kathy, Pam and I would drive down and back in one day. As the date drew near one problem arose, I had begun my second week of chemotherapy treatment scheduled the day before we were to leave for New York. Since everything was set up, I went for the chemo treatment and then hoped I would not get sick on the ride down, during the interview or on the ride home.

Life's Not Always a Day at the Beach

That next morning we all arrived at MSL at 6 a.m., loaded the van and off we went to Manhattan. As usual, I sat in front, Pam in the back and Kathy drove. The trip down was uneventful; we arrived in 3 and one-half hours and started looking for the Statue of Liberty and a place to tape the opens and closes to the show.

We parked in an underground parking garage, which had about 6 inches of room to navigate through; thankfully, I wasn't driving. We unloaded what we needed for equipment and headed over to the harbor across from the Statue of Liberty. Lots of people were hanging around, talking, eating, playing music, which complicated the shoot. We set up at the end of the walkway as far away from people as we could get, (which wasn't really far enough) but we taped the opens and closes in the overpowering sun, and headed back to the car to find the Times Building.

After driving around and realizing the GPS did not work very well with all the tall buildings, we found another underground parking garage, pulled in, unloaded the equipment and handed over the keys to the attendant. You really have to be very trusting when you try to park in Manhattan. Once we arrived in the Times building we were informed that we could not go up in the main elevator because our cart was too big, and that we had to wait for the Bomb Sniffing dog to check out our equipment. I guess they thought we were a trio of crazy women that were going to blow up the Times Building. So we waited, waited, and waited.

Meanwhile the Chemo was getting the better of me; I was feeling sick and standing around did not help. The only bright side to the wait was the Bomb Sniffing dog was a beautiful black lab. The dog sniffed all our bags,

Statue of Liberty
Photo by Paul R. Villare, III

Memorizing my script for
MSL Ed Forum: Moving Up in America

Life's Not Always a Day at the Beach

found out we were bomb-free and security took us up the back elevator to the floor and conference room to set up in. Or not? Kathy and Pam began to move things around and set up the interview, when an employee burst in and informed us that we were in the wrong room; that they had a big meeting scheduled for this room and we had to get out. So everything stopped and once again we waited. By now I was really not feeling well. We were asked to leave the room, and stand outside it while they set up for their meeting. Kathy was not at all happy about the whole ordeal and pulled out a chair from the room for me to sit on to WAIT!

Finally, someone walked us to another conference room, and once again time to set up. So, here we are in downtown Manhattan and we once again are taken to a dark, windowless room to shoot an interview. I could tell Kathy was not happy. But as usual we made the best of it. We set up the room and began to wait - - and wait some more. I started to feel real sick because we had not eaten and it was getting late. Kathy ran around and found crackers and something for me to drink. After another hour, Rana showed up. The interview went well; she answered all my questions and then left. We began the process of packing up and moving out. By this time, most of the people had gone home so we had to wait for someone to take us downstairs to exit the building. This person did not make us go down the back elevator; they did not even know there was one. Pam was to drive us home, and said we would stop for food once we got outside the city. Kathy remembered she gave me crackers before we left so we ate those while we tried to get out of the city. The GPS which is guiding us home reminded us again that it was having trouble reaching the satellite signal because of all the tall buildings. I'm close to passing out now. From the back seat, Kathy gets us out to the roadway we came in

TV TRIPS WORTH MENTIONING

on and Pam takes it from there. Naturally, we hit massive traffic getting out of the city but we got through it and headed for home. One problem: there is nowhere to eat right outside the city. It isn't until we hit Connecticut late that night that we pull off for "lunch".

"SAVE THE TIGERS"

The Plight of the Tigers in the U.S. began with a frantic call from a former MSL Student, Rose Church who was a Volunteer Lawyer at the Ian Somerhalder Foundation. Rose Church had been working on an international animal abuse case when she received a call about a full grown tiger being kept at a truck stop in a small cement cage. Nowhere to roam, nowhere to hide, this magnificent animal lives a miserable life in captivity. This began Rose's research into other tigers being kept as backyard pets in the U.S. Rose called me about this problem and we sprang into action. First, Rose and I read and researched all state and federal law pertaining to the keeping of exotic animals as pets (Tigers in particular). We talked with a number of sanctuaries and contacted Federal Senators and Representatives. Rose set up a non-profit organization named "World Council for Animal Rights" in case funds would be needed to move tigers from one location to another. We then decided that a meeting of a group of Animal Welfare Organization was needed to help with this issue. Rose began working on setting up the date, and who should attend; this meeting would be held at the International Fund for Animal Welfare (IFAW) office in Washington D.C. I co-teach an Animal Rights course at MSL with Holly Vietzke. We then enlisted the help of 2 students. These students worked 8 - 20 hours a week on research and preparation for the meeting in Washington D.C. After planning the meeting, it was decided that a show should be produced to help with public awareness.

The thought was to have animal welfare organizations pressure the Fish and Wildlife service to close the generic tiger loop by offering a public comment period.

The generic tiger loophole allows inbred and cross bred tigers to be treated as if they are not "real tigers". These generic tigers have not been given the same legal protection as purebred tigers and thus have been bred extensively to provide pay-to-play schemes where animal exhibitors charge a fee to let the public pet or play with tiger cubs.

More than ten times as many people spoke out in favor of protecting all tigers than exploiters did to create this loophole.

Holly Vietzke, Rose Church, and I began an immediate campaign to inform the public of this dangerous and pressing problem by writing an article titled "Free Tony the Tiger" which was sent to all newspapers and websites to run. (see appendix)

It was decided that we would head down to D.C. for the meeting and take Pam and Kathy with us to tape interviews so that we could produce a program we could distribute across the country to inform everyone about the problem.

I began booking flights and setting up the van rental. My mind must have been elsewhere when I booked flights for Kathy and Pam because instead of coming home the same day we flew down, I had booked them on flights coming home on a different day. Kathy came laughing into my office saying if her brother Paul was

Victor Vanderlinden, Holly Veitzke, Katelyn Romano in front of The White House

Tiger and Cub

Life's Not Always a Day at the Beach

going to be around, she would not mind hanging out in D.C., but we would have to drive ourselves back to Baltimore if she stayed on, so she fixed our reservation.

On July 25th, we had an early morning flight to Washington D.C. One by one everyone began showing up for the flight. I rode in with Holly.

When I got to the airport, Kathy informed me my friend had been calling her, telling her she would have to come back out through security to get paperwork that he was bringing, assuming I had forgotten it. There was no possible way she could exit. The line was hours long. The calls kept coming and she kept ignoring them.

Everyone arrived at the gate expect Pam, no one saw her and Kathy tried to call her a few times. We began boarding-still no Pam and no answer on her phone. The door on the plane closed without her and we were off.

We arrived in Baltimore, picked up the luggage and then headed to the rental car location via the shuttle. We loaded the rental van and headed off to D.C. for the meeting. We ran into the usual Baltimore-D.C. traffic, but we found our address and Kathy dropped us off and went to park the van.

Kathy started setting up for interviews in one of the empty rooms. She finally heard from Pam, who forgot to bring her boarding pass and they could not find her reservation when she checked in at the front counter. Although she was on time to the airport, by the time they found the reservation the plane had left. To add to the drama, she forgot her cell phone at home. She had to take a taxi from Baltimore to D.C.

TV TRIPS WORTH MENTIONING

Our first interview was with Carol Baskin, Founder and CEO of Big Cat Rescue Sanctuary. Then I went back to the meeting and Kathy and Pam moved to another location so Holly could interview Nathan Herschler, an attorney and international operations manager with International Fund for Animal Welfare.

It was getting late and I still wanted Holly to interview the two interns that came with us with the White House as their backdrop. We packed up the equipment and headed to the garage for the van. One problem: Kathy forgot where she parked, but after a few minutes of walking around, she found the van, climbed in and off we headed to find the White House. Naturally, there was nowhere to park so I told Kathy to double park; I would wait in the van while they shot the interview. Now this problem quickly came to mind: I could not have driven this van through Washington D.C. if my life depended on it, so if the police arrived, I was in trouble.

When we finished, we all climbed into the van and back to Baltimore we went. Just about everyone was falling asleep on the way back. Back at the rental car terminal, we all loaded our gear on the shuttle bus when Kathy realized she left her cell phone in the van and got off to go get it.

We rushed to the airport like firemen, but the plane was delayed. Kathy arrived on the next shuttle and asked why we were all standing around. We explained the delay, and decided we would go through security and find somewhere to eat until our flight.

For this show we also set up interviews with Adam M. Roberts, the Executive Vice President of Born Free USA, who came to the school, and we took a trip down to

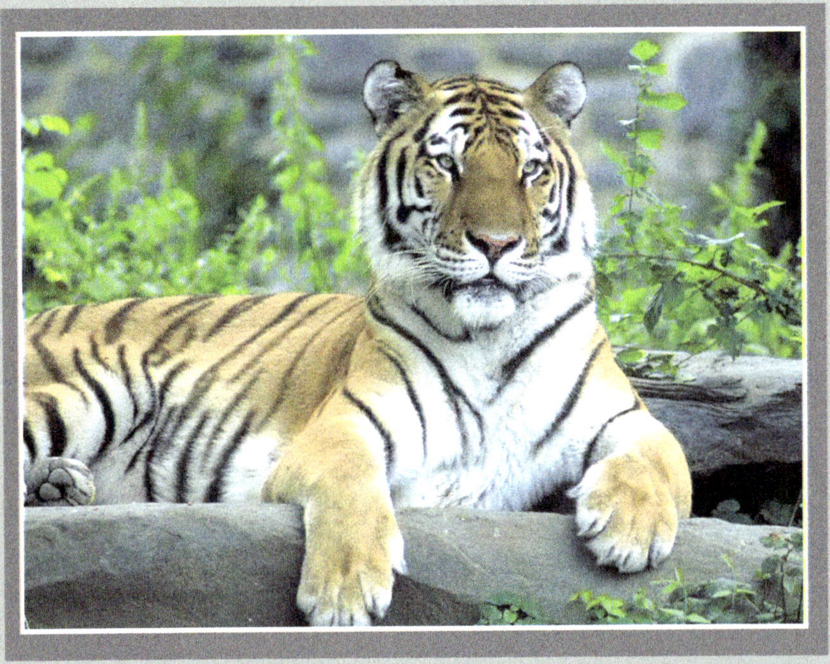

TV TRIPS WORTH MENTIONING

Cape Cod to shoot interviews with Ian Robinson, a veterinarian and International Fund for Animal Welfare's Emergency Relief, Program Director, Grace Ge Gabriel, the Regional Director, International Fund for Animal Welfare- Asia and Rose Church, Volunteer Lawyer-Ian Somerhalder Foundation and the CEO of World Council for Animal Rights.

On a very sad note, as we were in our final edit, the tragedy at Zanesville Ohio happened. On Wednesday, October 19, 2011, 56 exotic animals- lions, tigers, bears, giraffes and wolves-were freed from their captivity at a rural residence outside Zanesville, Ohio. Police reported the animals' "owner," 62-year-old Terry Thompson, let the animals out of their cages before he killed himself. When the carnage was over, 49 animals were slaughtered, including 18 Bengal tigers, 17 lions, six black bears, a pair of grizzlies, three mountain lions, two wolves and a baboon.

Only six animals - a grizzly bear, three leopards, and two monkeys -- were captured alive and taken to the Columbus Zoo and Aquarium. We now had the attention of everyone, including our Senators, who had ignored our pleas earlier.

Apollo, Sasha and Me

THE ANIMAL ADVOCATE

The greatness of a nation can be judged by the way its animals are treated.
                                    Mahatma Gandhi

     When my mother died I remember thinking that I would never be happy again. I was overcome with grief; I thought it would be impossible for me to truly feel light-hearted ever. But somehow, I put a smile on my face like mom taught me, and the pain subsided and I went about my life in a happy but different way. Four years later, when dad died after a horrific battle with cancer, again I was grief-stricken, but this time I was relieved by his death - - because his pain was over. So very sad, but relieved. And my life now has been good.

Life's Not Always a Day at the Beach

Hurricane Katrina

It was a beautiful day. I drove to the law school in my convertible with the top down, but when I turned on news radio instantly the sun left the sky. I was chilled to the bone. "How can the sun shine so brightly here in Boston, while others cry in pain and grief in New Orleans?" I had thought. Reports of looting, raping of women, mayhem, disorder. And then I heard about the plight of the animals - - the trusted, loyal family pets. Abandoned. Starving. Drowning. Many of the animals were not rescued and in fact were deliberately left behind. There were at least 250,000 of them needing rescue and many thousands more in need of homes.

Often people had to choose between their own safety or their pet's. To forbid people access to safety and shelter if their companion animal clung to their side was not a choice a person in a civilized society ought to have to make. Clearly, not in America. I had to shut off the radio.

I went to my office at MSL. Like always, The New York Times was in my box. And on the front page was a picture of the horror I was trying to escape - - a woman being forced to separate from her german shepard dog. It was more than I could bear to see.

As a professor of law and specifically of animal law, I begin the course with a discussion of the legal status of animals. I teach law students that animals are seen as property - - the equivalent of a piece of furniture or clock or television or some other inanimate object despite the fact they experience pain and emotion. I urge them to try to foster change to work to reclassify animals as beings. Perhaps, then they won't be left behind to be swept away

THE ANIMAL ADVOCATE

by the water ....

When the disaster struck New Orleans, I did what I could. I sent money to the Red Cross. I donated blood. I sent clothes to a shelter. The appeal was intense and like so many other Americans, I responded to help the people. It was not easy to help the animals. You had to engage in a search as to where to donate. Query: Why wasn't that front page as well?

Years have passed since I saw the picture of the poor german shepard. I am haunted - - wondering if the dog was saved. Was it ever reunited with its companion? What I read and what I saw was worse than the plight of people in third world countries. And this is mighty America. So this disaster, although not personal to me, leaves me restless and unsettled. The feelings do not pass. Pets are so much more than a piece of furniture. They depend on us for protection in times of danger. I can tell you for sure, if I were one of the holdouts in New Orleans, under no circumstances would I leave without my two dogs. I owe them that much.

So, those of us who teach animal law know that one pervasive theme that resonates throughout our courses is American society's convenient classification of animals as property. Oftentimes, as expressed in existing law, pets are worth nothing more than a piece of merchandise --and a low priced one at that. That treatment inevitably leads to the most basic question of: how a society as great as ours can equate life - any life, much less woman's best friend -with a piece of furniture or even the latest iPhone? We all must find a way to answer the question debated in our classrooms and scholarly research. How can the law better protect our animals, our pets, and yes, our companions, when they most need sanctuary from harm's way?

FEMA New Orleans, LA,
September 8, 2005 -- Stray dogs and other
animals found in areas impacted
by Hurricane Katrina

THE ANIMAL ADVOCATE

Legal textbooks on animal rights are replete with judicial decisions that, in case after case, make all too clear that the law does nothing to genuinely protect animals. It certainly does not recognize their true value and special place in our homes. Our legal system fails to recognize the bond between us and our pets; when that bond has been severed, our legal system completely fails to compensate for that loss. Until recently, I have been telling my students that societal attitudes toward animals are changing. "A brighter day is coming," I tell them. I assure them that, over time, the status of our companion animals will evolve into one that is marked by compassion and humaneness, and that our laws will reflect that new status.

But Hurricane Katrina has shaken up my professorial prophesying. The stories and images have been unbearable. Years after Hurricane Katrina, I still see people clinging to their companion animals on the top of their roofs and then being forcibly separated. I still see refugees escaping with their pets to designated bus pick-up areas, only to be commanded to abandon their pets or remain behind with them and in danger. To forbid people access to safety and shelter when they and their pets are giving deep emotional support to each other is unconscionable. This is all the more so in our most prosperous of countries. We learned of animals abandoned, drowned, starved, and left for dead ... perhaps 250,000 in all.

The loss of these lives and the separation of thousands of others from their human companions have given urgency to the need to reclassify, legally, the status of domestic animals from property to beings. Defining companion animals as property is morally wrong and prevents their full protection.

Life's Not Always a Day at the Beach

Legislation has now been enacted that mandates pets be included in evacuations. U.S. Congressman Barney Frank of Massachusetts was one of the sponsors of a federal bill that requires provisions for pets and service animals in disaster plans in order for those plans to qualify the state or municipality for federal emergency funding. This is, of course, to be praised, but it's too late to save the animals that perished during the hurricane and its aftermath. We still need more progressive legislation to reflect the role of a companion animal's place in the family and within society.

Also, we need to vigorously prosecute those who abuse, neglect, or harm animals. The good news is that penalties for these actions are now more severe. The not-so-good news is that many police chiefs and district attorneys do not pursue these stronger penalties because they still have a mindset that an animal is property with no rights and little protection under the law.

Those of us who care about the welfare of animals must bring about a change regarding the classification of "standing" in animal cases. Standing is a legal term that is defined as a right to initiate a lawsuit. Historically, someone seeking relief on behalf of a harmed animal has very little power to so do. Lawsuits could be more easily advanced on behalf of animals if the law in all states was changed to provide standing to assert claims on behalf of their companions.

There is resistance to this from commercial interests, which brand animals as chattel. Animals are defined as property because it is convenient...and profitable. This allows them to be exploited, harmed, and used for experimentation and entertainment, all with impunity.

THE ANIMAL ADVOCATE

Our unfortunate history shows that slaves, women, and children were previously treated as property. The law was changed to stop this deplorable treatment. It is time to reclassify the legal status of companion animals.

Veterinary services provided by FEMA's VMAT teams

Jackson Falls, Jackson, NH

THE FLOOD

I certainly wouldn't say that my life is a disaster, but there have been moments where I have felt like that.
                                         Duncan Sheik

    I had been a law professor for over twenty-five years and I never remembered anyone knocking on the classroom door. So, when I heard the soft knocking and went to the door, I had an inkling my assistant, Laura, was not bringing me good news. "Everything is o.k., and your dogs are fine, but you need to go home right away because water is pouring from your walls and ceilings". I quickly looked outside. It's a bright, sunny day, how is this possible? Broken pipe? Not good whatever the cause.

    I quickly headed for home, running from the classroom to the car. I passed my colleague, Paula, who asked what was wrong, so I told her what I knew. Paula called her husband, Greg, who lives nearby. When I pulled up

Life's Not Always a Day at the Beach

in my driveway, Greg was exiting my house, fleeing my house - - like a thief in the night. My dogs did not welcome his presence and he couldn't get out fast enough. Fortunately, Greg made his way through my house and turned off the water supply. Ceilings were beginning to cave in, and water filled the basement. My dog Whitey thought it was great fun to have water pouring on him while he stood in the kitchen. My dog Winnie was terrorized and running in circles, waiting for the house to collapse I'm sure.

In the end, not everything was destroyed, but many items were; and all my clothes were soaking wet out on the lawn - - I guess I would not be making my cousin's wedding the next day. Walls were taken down, floors taken up and the only usable room was part of the living room. Huge fans were installed to dry the house which sounded like helicopters landed in every room. We put a mattress on the floor and used it as a bed, kitchen table, and dressing room. Finally the dogs and I moved to a hotel for the duration of the repairs. Each day though, I would bring the dogs to the yard at the house while I went to work. I was tied to my computer watching the weather forecast hour by hour. Over all, we survived this test and about four months later everything was back to normal, at least for the time being.

Sitting on the rocks in *Jackson Falls* interviewing Tom Ryan author of *Following Atticus: Forty-Eight High Peaks, One Little Dog, and an Extraordinary Friendship*

Michael L. Coyne, Esq.
Dean and Professor
The Massachusetts School of Law at Andover

THE GREAT LAND GRAB

Michael L. Coyne and Diane Sullivan,
Professors of Law
at the Massachusetts School of Law at Andover.

Mom was right. You reap what you sow. Since last year when the Supreme Court decided Kelo v. The City of New London, there has been a threefold increase nationally in the use of the draconian measure of eminent domain. In Kelo, the United States Supreme Court empowered the biggest land grab in our nation's history unless you include our acquisition of Texas and California. The beneficiaries of this latest land grab, as Justice O'Connor predicted in her dissent in Kelo, are "those citizens with disproportionate influence and power in the political process including large corporations and development firms".

Life's Not Always a Day at the Beach

Many state legislatures have tried to curb the exponential rise in the use of eminent domain following the Kelo decision. In the last year, twenty-eight states have added new protections against the broad use of eminent domain. More states need to develop better safeguards against the seizure of private property by the government, especially where it comes at the expense of marginalized groups.

The rule of law should be applied equally to the powerless and the powerful. It should be applied equally to the poor and working class and to those who don't give a whit about the poor. Time and time again, the Justices of the Supreme Court show us that they are so divorced from the real world that it matters little to them how their decision affects the lives of ordinary men and women; that the facts matter little and instead intellectual ideas and theories are their primary concern. However, the law cannot be divorced from the lives of the individuals it affects.

More state legislatures and state supreme courts must act to prevent further displacement of the working class. Those of us who teach law know that the law illuminates how real people conduct themselves and one cannot teach it with integrity, if it is divorced from humanity. Families whose lives continue to be disrupted in the name of progress deserve to be treated honorably and fairly. They ask for nothing more, and they deserve nothing less.

The 5th Amendment to the United States Constitution provides that private property will not be taken for public use without just compensation. All communities covet economic prosperity but eminent domain inflicts indignity upon the least politically powerful and disproportionately impacts poor and minority communities.

THE GREAT LAND GRAB

The power of eminent domain is useful in revitalizing many cities and towns. The continuing economic revival of many of New England's communities is essential for our region to prosper but state supreme courts and state legislatures must place reasonable limits on the use of the extraordinary power of eminent domain to take an individual's home and destroy communities for the purposes of private development. For their pain, the loss of homes, and their cherished memories, homeowners often receive a mere pittance despite the constitutional guarantee of just compensation. The government's unwanted actions should never place the homeowner in financial peril.

The notion of just compensation may matter little to justices of the Supreme Court as they go to and from work in their chauffeur-driven vehicles, but to the poor and working class the value of their homes is often their single biggest asset. At a minimum, homeowners should be entitled to both the fair market value of their homes and any relocation costs needed to put them as close to the same situation they were in before the city forced them to leave. A forward thinking interpretation might also include the increased value of the land as part of the new development so that the landowner will benefit from the loss of his home instead of politically connected developers. It is immoral to take from the poor and working class to serve the rich.

There may be some cause for hope, however. Recently the Ohio Supreme Court ruled unanimously that, under its constitution, private property could not be seized for private development despite the claims of public officials that the development would benefit the community. Twenty-eight states now provide additional protections that would not have existed if not for the backlash

Life's Not Always a Day at the Beach

from the Kelo decision. Let us hope that more protections follow and more communities recognize that when they seize property by eminent domain they are not just taking, as Justice Maureen O'Connor of the Ohio Supreme Court said, a "plot of cold sod" but they are taking a "home, a place where ancestors toiled, where families were raised, where memories were made." The Ohio Supreme Court found that our property rights are integral aspects of our theory of democracy and notions of liberty. Let us be forever vigilant to insure our democracy and liberty are protected.

When Mike Coyne and I heard about this case, and spoke in opposition, never did I believe I would be a victim of eminent domain. Less than one week later, I received a call from the Massachusetts Highway Department to meet at my property. The state had decided to expand the road adjacent to my house, put in a major intersection and an access lane. They told me I had no choice. I had to take down my fence, which they argued at a few points impinged on state property, although I disagreed. Initially, I refused to take it down because that was my dog's yard, and it cost me well over $10,000 to fence it in. The state was insistent – take down the fence or we'll plow it down, which they ultimately did. They also took a part of my land, promising reimbursement, which I had to hire a lawyer to recoup the pittance. They paid a few thousand dollars only. I had to pay for a new fence myself – costing me $22,000.00 out of pocket. They took down my trees, decimated my yard, and left me in tears to reconstruct my home, and that was only the beginning. The way the state redesigned the road, during every rainstorm my basement flooded. After several storms with days of hauling buckets, up and down the stairs, sometimes for twelve hours at a time to get bailed out, until I could do no more, I eventually had to hire a professional company

THE GREAT LAND GRAB

to build wells and drains to solve the problem. "Just compensation"? I don't think so!

Apollo enjoying his fenced in yard.

Runner in training!

Citgo Sign, Kenmore Square, Boston MA

THE BOSTON MARATHON

I had as many doubts as anyone else. Standing on the starting line we are all cowards.
    Alberto Salazar – three time winner
        of the NYC Marathon.

I began running when I was 18 and finished my first marathon in 1975 only a year or two after women were allowed to run in the Boston Marathon. I had watched the running of the Boston Marathon and was dismayed that someone I knew in high school was a top contender to win. Randy Thomas was a little ahead of me in school, but in his early high school years he was known as "Fitchburg Fats" - - a player on our beloved high school football team. So I thought if Randy is a top contender, then I probably could win - - really what was I thinking? I've run dozens of marathons, some official, some unofficial, one in a little over 3 hours, many in nearly 5 hours. This one tells my experiences:

Life's Not Always a Day at the Beach

It's 6:00 a.m. and I lay awake wondering if I can make the trek from Hopkinton to Boston today.

I've been training since Labor Day (nearly seven months) in the dark, the rain, the snow, the fog, and the sub-zero weather, but I'm not certain it's enough. Imagine that, seventy to 100 miles a week, yet I'm frightened I won't make it. I fear that I might crash and burn out there on the course. But, I'm committed. I've told the world (including my law students) I'm running today and more importantly, I've told myself.

It's high noon and we're off, running the road to Boston. The first mile's pace is slow and downhill and I think maybe this run won't be so bad after all.

The crowd is great. I can't determine if they came to see the winner, Johnny Kelly, or maybe even me, because they haven't stopped cheering since the first runner went by. The young and the old extend their hands, wanting just to touch us -- to wish us luck. Somehow, I know I will need a lot of luck today and a lot of support from this crowd; and for the first ten miles they don't disappoint me. They clap, they cheer, they line the streets with water and oranges and all the encouragement they can muster. They see my sweatshirt and shout: "Go for it Mass. School of Law; we're with you!" Boy, teaching law is a lot easier than this, but no one cheers for you.

And so, we run through Ashland, then Framingham and into Wellesley. Just when I begin to think I can do this, (before sunset at least) it begins to rain. If you are a top-seeded runner, the rain won't be much of a problem because you are entering Cleveland Circle now. But for me, I begin to wonder if I can run 13 miles in the pouring rain. The crowd begins to go home and I think maybe

THE BOSTON MARATHON

I should join them. By mile 14, I feel my form start to deteriorate. My right hip hurts and I'm starting to freeze. Man, am I a mess.

I keep on running; left, right, left. I keep going. I'm approaching Newton now with the hills up ahead. My hands are numb from the cold and my feet aren't far behind. As I run by the Red Cross station, a worker yells out: "Are you okay? Need anything out there?"

Well, one hill down, two more to go. I'm hopeful now. I will make it to Boston.

It's been pouring for hours now, the crowd is gone, and at the water station no one is working except the clean-up crew sweeping up the mess. The runners have come and gone. But hey - what about me? I need water too, and boy would I kill for a slice of orange. Keep running; left, right, left. . .

Although I'm not overly religious, at mile 21, I begin to pray and make the promise of the hopeless. "Dear God, I'm not certain I can make another mile. But if you help me out, carry me into Boston, I promise I'll be good for the rest of my life." Keep running; left, right, left. . .

Then I pray the prayer of the truly desperate. "Okay God, if you do me this one favor, I'll go to church every Sunday. I'll do anything you ask, if you do me this one little favor." Left, right, left. . .

"Yahoo!" There it is! The Citgo sign -- only a mile or so to go. So, as I shuffle up the overpass, I realize for the first time I'm going to make it. And finally, there it is: the beautiful Prudential Tower. I made it. Through the hills, the rain, and the wall of pain. "I made it! I made it!"

Ryan, Korey and Me

THE HOCKEY AUNT

When my nephew Ryan took up dek hockey as a youngster, my parents were thrilled. We would take mom in her wheelchair to see her eldest grandson at age four play, just as she had watched her youngest son, Michael. Ryan is a sweet kid, so he did not appear aggressive enough or she simply thought she could improve his game because I found out she bribed Ryan. Mom promised Ryan $1.00 every time he touched the puck during his second game. Imagine that, bribing her own grandson. Little did she imagine or maybe she did, that Ryan would go on to be a captain of his high school ice hockey Division 1 team at St. Bernard's High School. This was an impressive accomplishment for a kid who had never put on ice hockey skates until he was ten years old. Skating though is in our family genes, except for mine. I don't even know how to skate backwards. Ryan had this defensive move she would be proud of – he'd use his body in all layout to

Life's Not Always a Day at the Beach

stop pucks on the way to the net!

Ryan's hockey coach, Kevin, knew our family. He was the catcher when my brother Mike pitched to several little league victories. Rumor has it, he was at the house the night my brother fell through the attic ceiling leaving a hole in his ceiling, and smashing his desk top. Had Michael fallen six inches more to the left, he'd have fallen down a steep flight of stairs and probably would not have survived the fall. When Dad heard the loud bang, he yelled upstairs to the boys and said, "Stop wrestling". When Dad found out what happened, Mike was grounded and Kevin was ignored when he asked Dad if that was a bad night for him to sleep over.

My second nephew, Korey was born with a severe cleft palate and accompanying deformities. It was near impossible for him to drink his bottle as an infant, and he nearly starved to death. He has had nearly thirty operations to date, but they have never been able to close his palate. Korey has not let that get in his way.

Korey has followed his brother since he has been in diapers. He played dek hockey at two in diapers, and ice hockey at six with his brother. His small size has made him quick and his eye/hand coordination is unbelievable. He has used hockey to get himself back from each surgery. One year, after having surgery, the hospital discharged him late Christmas Eve so he could be home for Christmas. He arrived about 7:00 p.m. stitched and blood stained unable to yet eat any solid food. I turned down his bed, he opened up his hockey bag announcing he was playing in his game early the next morning on the 26th. Korey is my inspiration. He always has a positive attitude, despite overwhelming obstacles. Let me take you back to a few of his games.

THE HOCKEY AUNT

IT'S THE END OF THE GAME
THAT MATTERS MOST

In my house, you grew up loving sports. The Red Sox, Patriots, Celtics, and Bruins were members of our family. My brothers were hockey legends Orr and "Espo", and at ten years old, I fell deeply in love for the first time. To prove my love, I purchased a gold heart at Woolworths for 99 cents. On it, I had engraved my love's name -- "Yaz" (left fielder for the Boston Red Sox). I wore it for years.

In our home, watching sports huddled around the television was quality family time. Great moments in Boston sports history occupy some of my favorite childhood memories. The "comeback kids" of the '67 Sox, the big bad Bruins and later those celebrated 7 games between our Boston Celtics and the L.A. Lakers made many a family gathering just a bit more exciting. I was more mature then. An "I Hate the Lakers" tee shirt now replaced my "Yaz" heart.

All of those championships, last second victories and comebacks pale in comparison to memories of hockey games involving my nephews. For example, there were district and state championship games where their team would make what seemed to be an insurmountable comeback taking games to overtime and victory. I remember once praying for a miracle with three seconds on the clock and a one goal deficit. My prayers were answered because my nephew Korey believes in miracles, in hard work, in perseverance, and never, ever, giving up, as does my oldest nephew Ryan. Korey always believes the game will be won. He's from Boston, and Boston sports fans believe always the game will be won . . . even if our faith is not immediately rewarded. Some of his team's comebacks go right to the memory bank – next to the Sox sweeping the

Life's Not Always a Day at the Beach

next four games after being down three games to eliminate the Yankees, win the pennant and then the World Series.

So, when the whistle blew and the contest began for the Dek Hockey National Cadet Championship, I was positively sure my nephew's team – the local team – would win. After all, they had already defeated the opposing New Jersey team in the opening round 8 to 6 and the score really didn't represent how much our team dominated. They then won every game all the way to finals. Korey had been waiting for this day for well over a decade. And he planned to win and so did his teammates. So the win was inevitable. Right?

At the opening face-off, the Leominster kids rushed the net and scored quickly. They soon added to the lead. I sent text messages to absent family members of what I thought would be an impending victory. Despite Churchill's admonition to never give in . . . "never yield to the apparently overwhelming might of the enemy," the Leominster kids let New Jersey back into the game. In the end, New Jersey put one past the reach of the lunging goaltender and it was over. Leominster lost the National Championship game.

I sat frozen. I watched my nephew from the stands. He threw off his helmet. Next came the stick. I could only imagine how disappointed he was. He's been playing this game since he was a toddler chasing after his older brother, Ryan, and has been focused on this championship for years. I thought of how many games I've attended and never witnessed him display poor sportsmanship. Don't blow it now, Korey, I thought. He was steaming, literally and figuratively – he had played his heart out and lost. Now he was angry. Query: What does one say or

THE HOCKEY AUNT

do? Nothing. I chose to just sit quietly in the stands and watch. Alone. The crowd had filed out.

The teams then lined up to shake hands. A good tradition, I thought to myself. Korey was in the middle of the line, not his normal second place formation. He shook the hand of the goalie – the same hand that repeatedly robbed him of the winning goal. Next in line, was the opponent who scored the winning goal. Korey put out his hand. What happened next made me cry – Korey shook his hand, turned away and then turned back and put his arms around his competitor and hugged him. He then proceeded down the line hugging each and every player. His teammates then followed suit. What a visual, nearly 50 young men hugging each other. So, at the end of the game, the final result matters most.

Then there was Korey's semi-final championship high school ice hockey game when he was a junior in his High School. When they introduced the opponent, Littleton High School, I will confess I gave up the idea of going to the title game. As they called Littleton's starting five who skated forward, I thought we were in trouble – doomed to be exact. These guys were substantially bigger than "us". When the starting line-up for Fitchburg was announced, our players didn't come forward, but stayed with their teammates. So, our team, the Fitchburg team stood united and they believed the game could be won. Fitchburg always believes the game will be won. . .

My mind drifted back to a classroom at the Massachusetts School of Law where I am a law professor. It was the first day of a contracts class when I called randomly on a student - - Nick Carbone. Nick started to speak, while sitting in the last row at the back of the classroom. From the podium I asked him to stand

Life's Not Always a Day at the Beach

because lawyers stand while speaking I told him. He responded, "Professor, I can't. I'm in a wheelchair". Well, Nick, I responded then, please proceed." . . .

I watched Nick that semester maneuver his wheelchair through the snow, and if we think this has been a hard winter - - just ask Nick about hard. He knows all about it. He's from Fitchburg. Played hockey there I believe. He's on the Massachusetts School of Law Mock Court Trial Team as a Northeast regional winner competing for the Thurgood Marshall National Championship title in Houston, Texas, alongside a team from Harvard and another MSL team.. Not bad for a kid from Fitchburg.

Back to hockey. In the most exciting game I have ever witnessed, a small team with big dreams played their finest game of the season. Fitchburg's #22, Korey Wilson sparked the team with goals in the first and second period. The third period started with Fitchburg having two players in the penalty box. I thought Fitchburg was in real trouble because Littleton got to the semifinals on steam from their powerplay, but Fitchburg held them off. Unbelievable! Korey's goals then were followed up with two more from teammate Eric Legere. The goalie Finn, mastering then his fourth straight shutout - - took my breath away with his one-handed saves. The coaches should be applauded for providing the training and the discipline for hard work to bring a very young team to the title game.

These Fitchburg kids "played their hearts out". The defense played so hard, chasing down every opponent, that a few times they ran into each other - - literally. A freshman known as "D" played like a pro and #5, a soon-to-be ivy leaguer is as smart on the ice as he is off

Ryan and Korey with their Ball Hockey Team Mates

Korey skating for Fitchburg/Monty Tech High School

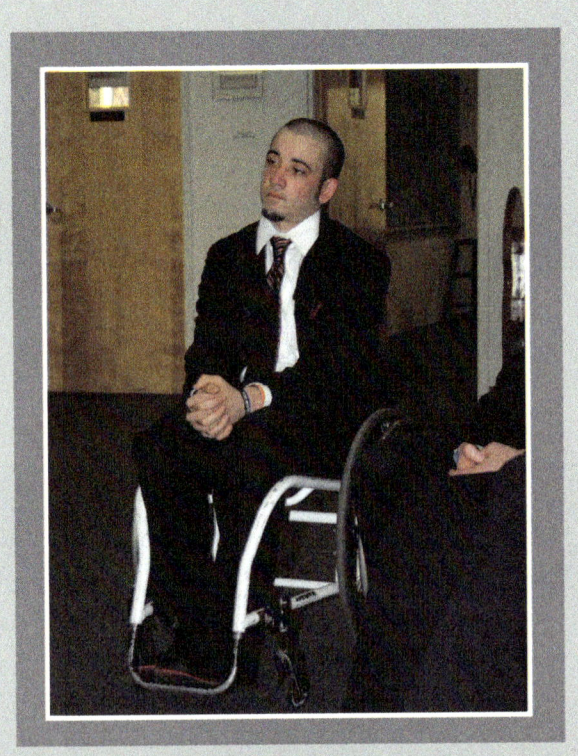

Nick Carbone

The Massachusetts School of Law Trial Teams

THE HOCKEY AUNT

the ice. And what about Kyle Peralta, making his debut on defense to take the spot of his injured teammate, Cordio. And Cory Paul, and Matt Lawrence were instrumental team players. I've never seen such team effort, except maybe from Nick Carbone and his trial team competing for a national title in Texas.

Next School Year

Once again, yesterday was a busy day at the Massachusetts School of law. Our trial team is away in New York competing against the trial teams of some of the most prestigious law schools in the Northeast. I'm anxious to hear of their success. I have a lot of things to do today to get ready for my contracts class so I arrived at school early.

However, first things first: I need to check the Sentinel and Enterprise Sports Page to see how the Red Raiders Hockey Team did.

I was not hopeful. This season has been one devastating injury after the next, including a season-ending injury to one of the team's stars, Eric Legere, minutes into the first game of the Bushnoe Tournament at Christmas.

That the Raiders ultimately won that tournament is nothing short of amazing, because if you saw the team minutes after Legere's injury, you would not have thought they could have pulled it off. But the coach called an early time out (despite the crowd's displeasure of using the only time out so early), and from that crucial point, the team played nearly flawless hockey. He must have told them to settle down, find each other and make it happen. They captured the crown (how sweet it was). As Babe Ruth said, "The way a team plays as a whole

Life's Not Always a Day at the Beach

determines its success."

But the season continued and the injuries mounted up. It seemed at times they were down to half a squad, but then they came back. Brandon Alicea was due back yesterday after a month out due to a shoulder injury. Then I heard this week that Cory Paul, another immense talent for the team, sustained a season-ending injury in practice and even I, the optimist, thought "that's it - - it is over". So, with trepidation I clicked on the sports page. "Red Raiders Erupt in Victory." This is too good to be true, I thought.

You see this is not just about a Fitchburg/Monty Tech. hockey game. It's about a group of kids with a dream. Apparently, they believe, as did Vince Lombardi, that "the price for success is hard work . . . (and in) applying the best of (themselves) to the task at hand." I admire all-out effort - - especially when the odds are overwhelmingly stacked against you. The Red Raiders' players seemed to understand when they put on their team jerseys, they represent not only their team, but all of us that have roots in and an affinity for Fitchburg; it is the name on the front of the shirt not the back, that is significant. So, when Emma, Wilson, and Casacca scored their goal or two or three, they did it for the Raiders and for us who care so much about the success of "all things Fitchburg". My parents worked in the mills in Fitchburg - - my father in the paper mill and my mother making ice skates. They taught me to succeed in life, dream big, work hard, play to win, and skate right through troubles when they piled up.

They believed Teddy Roosevelt:

The credit belongs to the man who is actually in the arena, whose face is marred .

THE HOCKEY AUNT

. . who strives valiantly . . . who, at best, knows in the end the triumph of high achievement, and who, at the worst, if he fails, at least fails while daring greatly, so that his place shall never be with those timid souls who know neither victory nor defeat."

DiGeronimo, Peralta, and the rest of the defense play so hard, game in and game out, chasing down every puck and opponent. Chapman, the goalie, has had a tough assignment -- keep his team in the game – especially with key offensive players down. The Fitchburg kids and coaches are to be admired. They continue to win, giving it their best effort against overwhelming odds. They haven't let the challenges of the season defeat them.

Nick Carbone, another Fitchburg High School graduate with ties to hockey, can also attest to responding positively when faced with obstacles. Nick is now in a wheelchair and is finishing his studies at the Massachusetts School of Law with significant achievements on our trial advocacy team. In January, he was also sworn in as a City Councilor for Fitchburg's Ward 5.

Now, if only the Massachusetts School of Law trial team can beat Harvard yet again.

Dean Michael L. Coyne,
New England Patriot Matthew Slater
and Producer/Director Kathy Villare

KATHY
THE PRODUCER
AUSTIN
THE STUDENT

When it is dark enough, you can see the stars.
                                  Ralph Waldo Emerson

When Kathy heard I was planning to undergo a stem cell transplant, she said she should follow me with a camera. "No! Absolutely not!" was my initial response. "End of subject," I said. So, that Sunday morning when I was walking my dogs at 6:00 a.m. in the dark, and my cell phone binged indicating a message, I knew it would not be a message of good tidings. It was from Kathy saying only that she had been thinking all night . . . For sure, this would not be good news. I called her. At the end of the conversation, I agreed to a show on the stem cell process, and I would be taped at crucial, pivotal points. How did she achieve this? Maybe because I realized if I can help others, I should. Maybe I want to do something to say thank you to Dr. Seldin and Dr. O'Connell. Last week,

Life's Not Always a Day at the Beach

a student came to see me because he was going to begin chemotherapy the next day, and he was so apprehensive he could not function. I was able to say to him, "close my door and let me tell you about my experience." It proved to be invaluable to him, and being a source to those who follow me is the right thing to do. After all, my role is an educator.

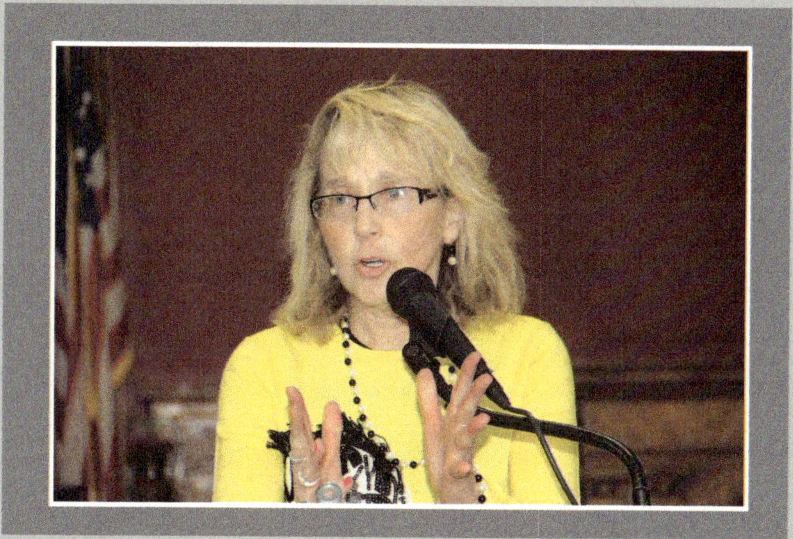

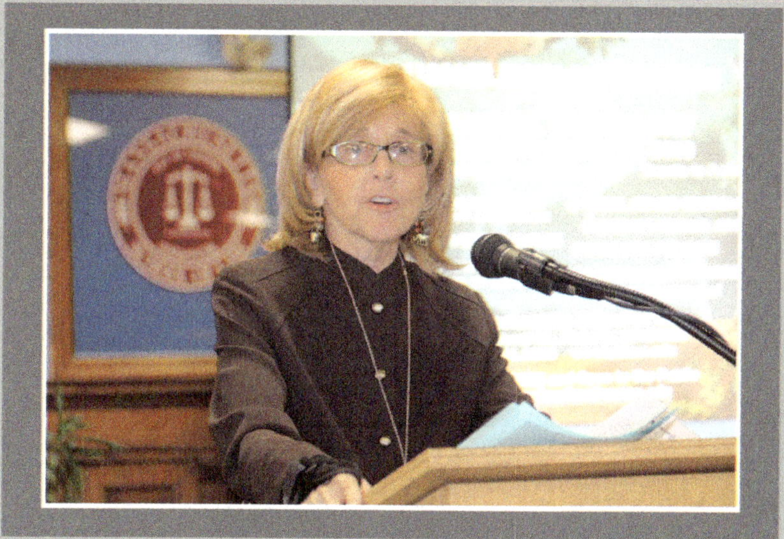

1969 Lucille Ball at work in
Here's Lucy

THE BIGGEST CHALLENGE OF ALL: THE STEM CELL TRANSPLANT PROCESS
-MY JOURNAL

Life is not easy for any of us. But what of that? We must have perseverance and above all confidence in ourselves. We must believe that we are gifted for something and that this thing must be attained.
　　　　　　　　　　　　　　　　　Marie Curie

Day 1   October 24th   The Masked Man
　　　I set my alarm for 4:40 a.m., just in case Whitey didn't get me up at the usual 4:00 a.m., but of course that was an unnecessary act. Despite his ailing leg, Whitey, Winnie, and I were out for our morning walk long before that buzzer was to go off. I was glad because I needed the extra time to figure "the wig" out, because I was still adamant about not looking in the mirror, being afraid of my hysteria when I saw my bald head.

　　　Lucille Ball's grandmother prohibited mirrors in the house Lucille Ball grew up in. Unlike Lucy, who

Life's Not Always a Day at the Beach

would have loved to see her reflection, after my hair was removed I could not, and would not, look at myself in a mirror. Having my head shaved to prevent the discomfort when the hair began falling out in two weeks was not easy for me. I stumbled trying to put my newly purchased wig on – in part because I would not look in the mirror, and because I have to wear a brace on my wrist now because of amyloid deposits in my wrist, and probably also because I was upset with the situation.

My mom lost her hair when she was sick and it was very hard on her. My dad said for over one year she would not leave the house. I now understand how she felt. My saving graces are my good friends, Laura and Kathy who came with me. My hairdresser Karen is a special person, and somehow we made it through with only a few tears. I still lack the courage to look at myself bald, though.

When my brother, Michael pulled into my driveway before 6:00 a.m. to take me to the hospital, I couldn't figure out why it was taking him so long to get out of his car. It wasn't until he emerged some ten minutes later in a mask that would scare anyone, that I got it. Mike had the sniffles three days ago and, unwilling to take any chance of spreading an infection to me, my cautious brother was figuring out how to put the mask on and no doubt he was sanitizing his car.

If you have to be really sick, Mike's the one you want to have at your side. He's smart, cautious, and funny - - he's an educated version of Dad. During the stem cell transplant, Mike kept a journal on line to keep my family, friends, and co-workers informed of the progress. Mike's entries are on page ii .

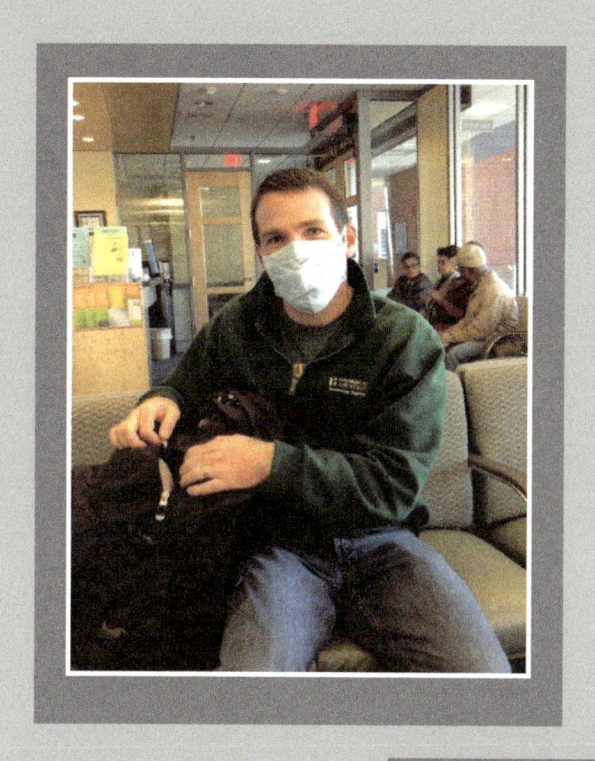

My brother Michael
The Masked Man!

Life's Not Always a Day at the Beach

When we arrived in Boston, we checked in at the hospital and sat in the waiting room. It was at this point Mike jumped up, pulled his sweatshirt over his head, lunged for his backpack, and ripped the mask off his cheeks and forehead. He had puddles of sweat rolling down his face. He was so hot that I think he was close to convulsions. The other patients watched wearily at his suspicious activity and my laughter. Mike couldn't understand why I was laughing hysterically, nor could anyone else, including the doctors standing nearby taking us in. I'm sure some patients feared he was a terrorist.

My day began with several viles of blood being taken. The technician complimented me on having beautiful hair color, asking if was natural. Oh my goodness - - not only is it not natural, it's a wig! The physical exam and heart test were uneventful, which was great, since the last time at check-in they were talking about taking me to surgery to paddle my heart into rhythm. I appreciated no crisis this time. We met with the nutritionist about the new neutropenic diet I would soon begin, not much of a problem for me, since I now ate this way normally. I was ordered on a neutropenic diet because the stamp cell transplant would effectively "kill" my immune system, and with a weakened immune system I needed this diet to protect against bacteria and other harmful organisms. Some rules I didn't mind, like no fresh fruits and vegetables. But I did mind the no soft-serve yogurt rule, though, so I knew I was heading to Andre's Yogurt as soon as I could exit Boston Medical. I can live without fresh vegetables and fruit – but frozen yogurt is a different matter altogether.

Our next meeting was with the stem cell transplant team, Dina Brauneis, RN NP-C, and with the stem cell Doctor, Dr. Sanchorawala. These two women are truly remarkable people: brilliant, nice, and high energy. Dina did not sugarcoat the procedure, and in truth, the stem cell collection and retransplant was to be a much trickier procedure than I thought. Stem cell transplant is a procedure that infuses healthy cells into the body to replace diseased cells. My autologous transplant consisted of capturing my own stem cells and re-transplanting them. Well, too late to turn back now. If, and only if, they cannot capture enough stem cells would this planned course of action terminate. Notwithstanding the last minute tick imbedded under my arm, all lights are green – bring it on!

Day 2 "My Heart Acts Up Again"

My brother and I arrived at 5:15 a.m. to have the double lumbar jugular central line placed in my neck and chest. This would serve as a port for the stem cell collection, melphalan chemotherapy stem cell infusion, blood draws, transfusions, just to name a few things. Mike again arrived looking like a terrorist in the mask he hasn't needed for days. The surgery went fine except that my heart went into A-fib, which means Atrial fibrillation, an irregular and rapid heart rate that causes poor blood flow. The doctors and nurses are extraordinarily skilled and it was really quite a procedure getting the lines inserted to sit on top of my heart. Everything worked out in the end, but the bruising to the chest lingered for days.

Day 3 "Family Stories"

So, I'm sore, bruised and bloody, but doing well. It was a long hospital day but the day ended with the growth factor injection to help multiply my stem cells. They are hoping to collect millions of stem cells from me next week. The medical team has warned me to expect bone pain, ankle and leg swelling, weight gain, and other delightful side effects.

Life's Not Always a Day at the Beach

It was a beautiful day out so when we finished at the hospital, Mike and I went across the street for Andre's yogurt. The small lunch area was full so we sat outside in the sunshine, in front of the Boston University Medical School and ate yogurt and told family stories. I told Mike about the time Dad banged on my door at two o'clock in the morning saying, "Wake up! Your brother may need a lawyer". I jolted up responding, "Dad, why would Mike need a lawyer? Are you crazy"? "There is blood on the hood of his car," he said. I laughed aloud, "Probably a bar fight over some girl". "Did you ask him?" "Yes," dad said, "he said something about hurting his hand." "He doesn't need a lawyer, Dad, go to sleep". "He could need one you know," dad shot back at me. Mike didn't recall this until I reminded him of the big old car he had one winter. Then he remembered. Mike said he got stuck in the snow, and when he was pushing the car out of the embankment he cut his hand on the grill. The police had stopped him too, he told me. Mike was shocked to hear what Dad thought. We both laughed until we sobered up thinking how my parents would take my being ill.

Day 4 "Batman's on the Roof"
Auntie Shaye (my sister's sister-in-law) stayed with me and took me into the hospital Saturday morning for more growth factor injections. Shaye was a nurse and has been part of our extended family for thirty years. Everyone should have a Shaye in their family. She will be my primary caregiver through the entire stem cell transplant process and through recovery at home. Her wonderful husband, Wally, is caring enough to encourage his wife to move with me to Boston for the next month. Wally sent me a note not to worry about him, he could take care of himself until I was healthy again. Aunt Shaye offers her love and time to anyone who needs her care. This is not the first time she's done this; she helped her Uncle Dave

Michael with Colin and Adian

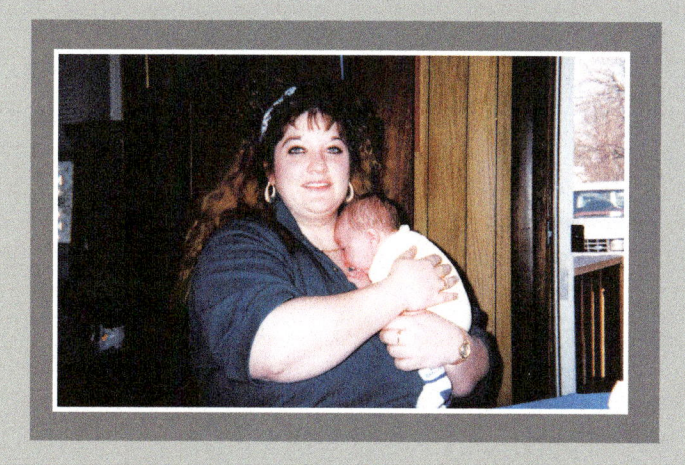

Aunt Shaye with Korey

through this process when the science was in its infancy.

On the ride into Boston our conversation was light. She reminded me of the first time she went to my family's home, and saw someone up on the roof dressed as Batman. She entered the house and said to my Dad, "Do you know you have Batman up on your roof, with cape and all." To which my father yells, "M-I-C-H-A-E-L!"

My visit was quick; vitals, weight, jugular check, and two growth factor injections, and away we went. Homeward bound.

That night, my dear friend, Gloria arrived to stay with me. I bet she regrets it. Gloria was pulling in my driveway while I was on the telephone with the on-call hematologist at Boston Medical Center. Severe headache, jaw, teeth, chest pain, pelvic pains, foot pain . . . "Can I take anything besides Tylenol"? I asked. "No," was the response. "The pain means the bones are swelling and that's what needs to happen. It really is good," he said. Sure it's not him, I thought. "And do not take any more Tylenol," the Doctor added. Suffer in silence, I thought. Great!

Quickly, the pain I was experiencing became so severe, I could not even sit and watch the Notre Dame vs. Oklahoma football game, and what a terrific game it was – one of the best ever! I began to pace, I continued pacing from pain until dawn when we headed back to Boston Medical for my next injection.

Day 5   Then There is the Hurricane
Nurse Jane was terrific. She put ice on my jaw to numb the teeth pain, heat on my head to dull the head pain, and called the hematologist, who took one look at me

and sent me home with pain medication, and a promise of relief the next day when my stem cells were extracted. As if life was not challenging enough, the predication of a hurricane striking the next day was the clincher. I was doubting my decision to go through the process. Dina, the Nurse Practitioner, informed me that I could withdraw my consent at any time in the process and I seriously contemplated that.

Day 6 "Thelma and Louise" Ride Again

Gloria and I headed to Boston Medical through the hurricane, with me in horrible pain, vomiting as we drove, and Gloria clenching the steering wheel to fight the wind and rain and stay on the road despite little visibility. I was so sick by the time we arrived I could not even sit up in the waiting room, which is a separate waiting room for stem cell transplants patients – meaning me – the transplant patient of the week. The day was a challenge for me and the medical team. I was sick. They were terrific, and India ran the stem cell machine without a murmur and collected 3.8 million stem cells on Day One! Yeah! The doctors were very concerned about my getting in the next day, as the hurricane continued. I promised to return, but the medical people thought I might need the help of the police because roads may be closed. One of our alums, who is Chief of Police, would have a plan if roads were closed.

Day 7 We Made it Into Boston

Sharon and I made it into Boston Medical. The stem cell collection went well; so well, a third day was not necessary. Today was very different because I felt much better. Thank goodness for my team. My colleague, Kathy, the producer of our television shows, came in to do a television taping, so the day ended up being a fun time, relatively speaking.

Life's Not Always a Day at the Beach

Day 8   Low Platelets, Lots of Yogurt
Today was to be uneventful – not quick – but uneventful. Since my stem cells were successfully collected and frozen, the only items on my medical calendar were blood draws, doctor evaluations, and so forth. My platelets were down but that was expected, so several hours later I was given the green light to leave and take the next day off from medical. Yeah! The only item on the agenda was frozen yogurt! I headed directly from the hospital to the yogurt shoppe and ate as much as humanly possible, because in a few days self-serve dairy was to be prohibited for a long time because of the bacteria.

Day 9   Day off – Heal the Soul
How wonderful to be normal, if only for a day. No medical today - - a wonderful day with just my dogs and visit with my sister.

Day 10   Back To Boston/My Wonderful Colleagues
The masked man has become normal again and arrived before 6:00 am. for our journey to the hospital. I'm on the rebound, plasma cell count is rising and I check out satisfactorily for the upcoming melphalan chemotherapy scheduled for Monday. When I returned back home later that day, I noticed some stuff from work on my kitchen table. Interesting, I thought, someone from work came here. Query: I wonder if my dogs ate them for an early dinner. It was then I decided I better check the house for any human remains, when I saw it: A banner from my colleagues wishing me well and words of love, complete with pictures. How am I so lucky to be in the company of these wonderful colleagues?

Day 11   Getting Ready to Leave My Dogs
Tomorrow I leave my dogs and my home to hopefully restore my health. My sister, Nancy will stay at

My MSL Family sending good wishes!

Laura Lussier and Kathy Perry
hanging the sign in my house.

Life's Not Always a Day at the Beach

my house to take care of them until I am well enough to move them to Boston with me. I need to make sure I have everything here that they need, and then pack myself for my stay in Boston. I am not looking forward to melphalan chemotherapy.

Day 12   Move to Boston
The move to Boston was not as bad as I thought it would be, mostly thanks to the terrific support of my brother and sister, and colleagues at work. Although, it was hard to leave my dogs, Nancy's message helped:

"....just take care of you and get the hell back home!!! I love you and need you back! I will try to treat your dogs like you do, but those are big shoes to fill... they will be fine.
See you soon!!! I will take special care of Miss Winnie".

Mike Coyne has given me permission-no, a directive-to sign off from work. I know I need to do that. MSL is just fine without me, and Amy Dimitriadis, my teaching assistant, had the class in good order. Words of encouragement came from Laura, Kathy, and Connie.

My neighbors, truly great people, came to wish me well, and brought an early Christmas gift. The boys wrote me the following cards, decorated with beads and smiley faces.

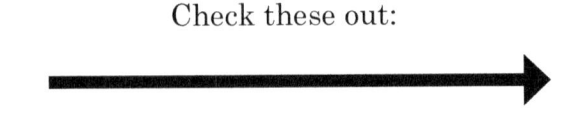

Check these out:

⟶

*Dear Diane,
I hope you get better soon, we really miss and love you, your new wig rocks!!!! I really really hope to see you soon,
Love,
Cory Nobile*

*Dear Diane,
I really love you and your wig. I wanted to know if I could help with anything.
Tyler*

Mike took me into Boston after we dealt with the flat tire on my car. My dear friend, Gloria met us in Boston to stay with me for the night. I had to pick up thousands of dollars worth of prescriptions at CVS. I wanted to walk since getting there by foot seemed easier and a more healthy way to pick up drugs. It probably was not the brightest decision to be walking through the streets of Boston carrying drugs, with my brother saying, "if we get jumped, scream. I'll take them on, you just run."

Day 13   Has it Come to This?
Since that day in August that I met with Dina about the upcoming stem cell transplant, I have been apprehensive of the ice treatment to be administered prior, during, and post melphalan. When Dina described the process, I felt it was beyond me. "Dina I just can't do that". Well, Dina convinced me that I could, but when I left our discussion about the stem cell process, I sat in the lobby and cried. My poor dear friend, Gloria seemed to be with me every time something went wrong, or I came up against my limits. I knew this would be bad and that somehow I'd get through it, but that didn't help much to survive the process. It was simply awful. In the end, I got through it thanks to help from Mike, Gloria, Kathy, and my nurse, Cynthia. The media representative of Boston Medical happened to be in the doorway, and said looking at all the people trying to help, "it really does take a village to get through this."

The best part of the day was meeting with Dr. Sanchorawala, the Medical Director of the stem cell transplant unit. Wow. I hit the jackpot with her - - most impressive doctor, and almost my neighbor. We had some laughs and we are on the same page about getting me home ASAP.

My wonderful infusion nurse, Cynthia just reminded me how far I have come: from the 4½ months of chemotherapy to the now successful, but painful, stem cell collection today. Then there was another horrific day of ice and melphalan, and then I could put this mountain behind me. In three days the medical team will re-infuse the frozen stem cells back into my body. It is quite probable that during the next two weeks I will be very sick, but I can deal with that. Home is ultimately on the horizon. When I ran marathons I would wait, wait, and wait to see, and then focus on seeing the Citgo sign, which meant the finish line was 1.2 miles away. Well, I cannot see the finish line yet, but in two weeks I will be looking. It is hard to imagine that I've gone from a woman who could do an ironman triathlon, to one who has pain and fatigue in her quads when she walks upstairs. Yesterday, I thought to myself: really has it come to this? But I like a challenge and should enjoy the process of getting to be healthy enough to at least run again. Even if I fall short, as long as I can teach my classes and walk my dogs, I shall be happy.

My friend, Gloria, who is here with me today, has a brother who has survived this disease – heart transplant with stem cells taken. Gloria's husband, Mark, spent months fighting for his life when a tractor tipped over onto him on his family's farm. Mark lost a leg plus he is now in a wheelchair. I have never seen Mark without a grin and an appreciation of life. I will use images of Mark and his positive attitude to get through round two of the stem cell collection scheduled for tomorrow.

Day 14   Torture By Ice

The ice treatment – stuffing your mouth continually with ice for 15 minutes before the high dose melphalan is given – 20 minutes during, and 15 minutes after (total

Life's Not Always a Day at the Beach

of 50 minutes continuous) is done to prevent mouth sores that would require hospitalization, and a morphine drip because the patient is unable to swallow or eat. The use of ice was discovered when a southern man who chewed tobacco came in for melphalan chemotherapy. He was forced to switch from tobacco to ice chips when he underwent this high dose melphalan. He was the only one who didn't develop the sores. Hence, the ice treatment.

I always thought I was tough, not as tough as my sister or brother, but tough nevertheless. I am not. The ice treatment nearly broke me. It was my worst physical experience and I almost couldn't tough it out. Without Mike, Kathy, Gloria, and Cynthia, I would not have done it. How lucky I am they supported me through this horrible ordeal? The ice treatment was torture, and if I were a soldier being shaken down I would spill the beans. Not a pleasant realization about yourself. My brother, Mike counted down the minutes and watched the clock as he helped with the ice. This was crucial to my psyche because the thought of doing one minute more than necessary was unbearable. Kathy and Gloria did yeomen's work to help me through the hour. But the ice treatment is now behind me. Whatever is ahead won't be as bad, and I do not intend to look in the rearview mirror AGAIN.

Day 15   Changing of the Guard
I've been up since 12:45 a.m. I couldn't sleep; must be the chemo treatment. I felt good. However, that lasted only for 15 minutes, because I then vomited up all my medication and headed to the hospital. Today included a medical check, blood draw, and catheter dressing change. In the end all went fine, and it was an early day. I have remained adamant about walking from the hotel to the hospital so I maintain some strength, but the approaching storm might impede that. Last week a hurricane, today a

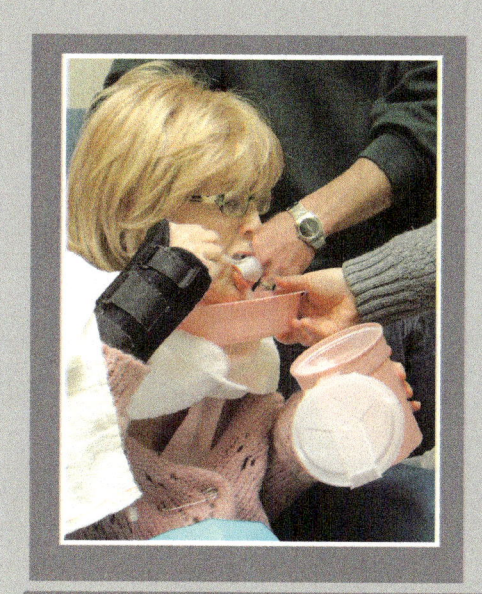

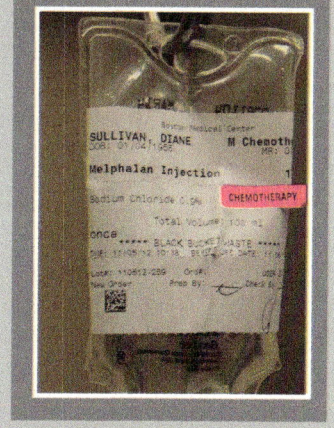

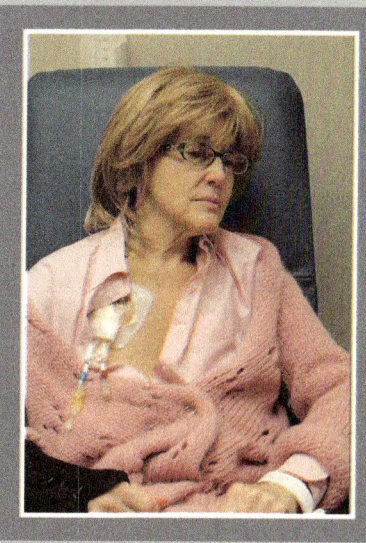

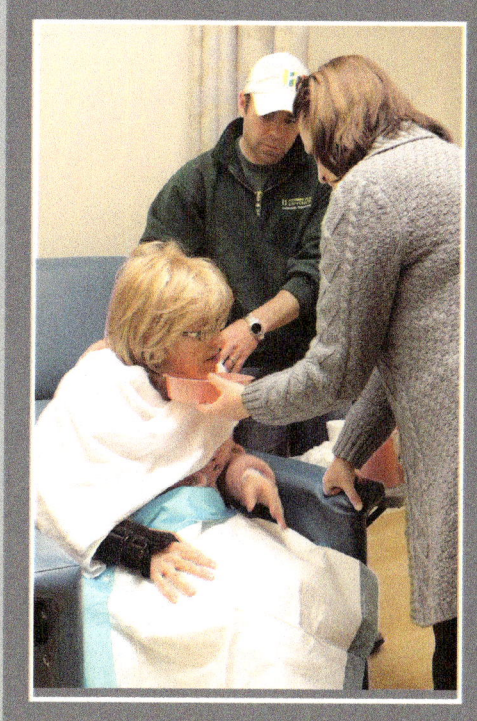

Ice and Chemo Day
and yes, it was as bad as I imagined!

Life's Not Always a Day at the Beach

nor'easter.

Auntie Shaye ("Sharon") has now come to stay with me until I go home. I could not be luckier. Sharon is such a devoted caretaker with a nursing background, and corresponding attention to detail.

Day 16   Infusion of My Frozen Stem Cells

I'm up at 4:00 a.m. ready to go, the only problem is that the infusion is not scheduled until 7:45 a.m. This will be a long day, but with Medical Director, Vaishali Sanchorawala, M.D. and Nurse Practitioner, Dina Brauneis, R.N., NP-C at my side, I am sure it will be entertaining as these two women are SIMPLY THE BEST. Dr. Sanchorawala lives near me and offers to stop by my house and pick up whatever I need. She is not only brilliant; she is a hoot! I feel as if Dina is my rope to life. My brother, Mike says he is always calm when Dina is in the room: competent, caring, smart, and witty, Dina looks like the good witch from Wicked, Glinda and it really fits her personality.

This morning I am surrounded by family - my brother, Sharon, my dear friend and television producer, Kathy, as well as my medical team. We began looking at my schedule: Kathy is planning for future shoots, and I am mentally counting the days to discharge. According to the medical chart, my first tentative date is Thursday the 29th of November (little do they know I'm planning earlier – like two weeks from Friday). The main problem is my brother – Mike, the warden. If Mike has his way, he will keep me here until my survival rate is 100% - which isn't going to happen. He loves and protects me, but I want to go home!

Dina and I

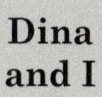

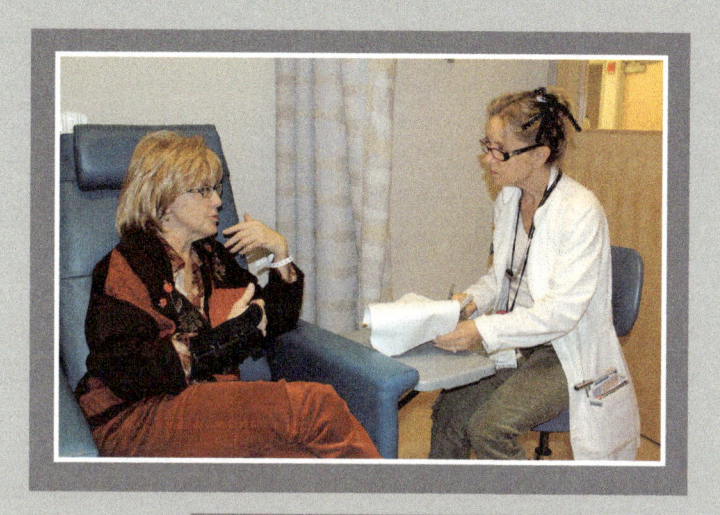

With Cynthia

Mark, Gloria and Me

Life's Not Always a Day at the Beach

Day 17 (Day + 1)
Hospital visit went well. I received my aranesp injection to promote cell growth and to give me antibiotics to help me get to normal. It is anticipated I will become very ill next week, but so far I feel pretty good.

Day 18 (Day + 2 from Stem Cell Infusion (counting up now))
Today, like future days, I will receive growth factor and antibiotics until my blood counts return to normal. So, I am off to the hospital getting what I need to return to normal and hopefully head home to my dogs in about three weeks – three long weeks (truth be told, I am counting on breaking the record – home in two, but we'll see).

Big night tonight. Notre Dame (9-0) takes on local rival Boston College. My only challenge is to be awake at 8:00 p.m. I remember one of the highlights of my father's life was when Mike took Dad to the Notre Dame/Boston College game. BC was slated to win with BC pressing on the second yard line. Yet, ND's super awesome defense held them for four. All of the Leamy family sat in their cars listening on the radio screaming for Dad.

Dean Larry Velvel (a Michigan fan) has been sending me text messages to the hospital:

> *"It looks like Notre Dame has a great shot at running the board as they say (winning all its games). There is nothing like having an excellent coach. I think it's likely that the fools in Ann Arbor could have gotten Kelly as head coach before he went to Sound Bend, but they chose not to, and later hired a guy whose record at the time was something like forty-eight wins and 50 loses - - can you believe it? More losses*

than wins. Meanwhile Notre Dame got itself a great coach".
(P.S. Not to mention the best defensive player in the land)

Day 19 (Day +3)   Growth Factor, Antibiotics, Patriots Kick off at 1:00 p.m. and Veterans Day

A Veteran's Day Tribute
Doing Right By Our Men and Women Soldiers
By Professors Diane M. Sullivan
and Michael L. Coyne
Massachusetts School of Law

Our fathers were members of "America's greatest generation". Each served his country when it called. Whether on the beaches of Europe in liberation of the concentration camps, or in service to this country for over 30 years as a member of America's oldest militia, the National Guard, they always answered the call. The time our families lost because of the scars our soldiers carry - - or because duty calls every weekend and then again during other kids summer vacations - - was the price we all pay for freedom we were taught. These were men of courage, integrity, service and most importantly to them and now us, men of their word.

America must start to do more for our returning wounded men and women. Women often fight our wars in Iraq and Afghanistan and a record number of these soldiers return badly wounded in need of promised medical care. In tribute to Veterans Day, President Obama stood at the tomb of the Unknown Soldier and proclaimed that America will not let veterans and their families down as "America is going to do right by them". So the question, Mr. President is when? When will

Washington D.C. Memorials

World War II

Korean War

Vietnam War

THE BIGGEST CHALLENGE OF ALL: THE STEM CELL TRANSPLANT PROCESS

America start doing right by its soldiers? Moreover, like America's greatest generation—are you a man of your word?

Too many men and women have gone off in service of their country only to return in futile search for appropriate care for the wounds they return with, whether they were inflicted by the gunfire of World War II, the bombs of the Korean War, our own Agent Orange of the Vietnam War or now the IED of the ragtag wars in Afghanistan and Iraq. America's greatest generation, their children and now grandchildren serve because we ask them to sacrifice their comfort and security for our comfort and security. Don't we owe those who return at least that much?

Visiting the VA hospital in the 60s left lasting images that will forever stain our memories. The promise of life long care meant traveling from one side of the city to the other in search of proper medical care. Upon arriving at that imposing building it was hard not to be impressed by the visible symbol of the promise that America would do right by its servicemen. But, promises after all are relatively cheap to make. That simplistic impression however, was quickly shattered. Ward after ward we walked in search of care. Returning Vietnam servicemen from the gritty neighborhoods of Boston lined up in bed after bed, perhaps 30-40 to a ward, many in visible pain laid in their hospital beds. No sons or daughters of Congressmen waited in those wards. After all, at the end of the day, the poor and middle class fight our wars. It's time we do right by them.

A veteran we know has been hit particularly hard. He was working, and like many of us, just getting along. His meager wages at a fast food restaurant barely allowed him to keep his head above water and the bill collectors at bay. He knew he would be unable to work much longer as he was losing his increasingly difficult struggle with his disabilities aggravated by the relentless aging process. He went to SSI to see if he would be eligible for assistance. SSI told him that as long as he was working they would not assess his eligibility for funding. He had to quit his job! He was afraid to quit because he would have insufficient money to exist. As time marched on, this disabled veteran could no longer work. His hands were "crippled up". Additionally, he suffers from posttraumatic stress disorder from his time in service to his country. With the assistance of strangers, he began the journey to qualify for benefits.

With no money, no transportation and limited education he, like so many disabled individuals, found the process overwhelming. Nevertheless, he soldiered on and completed all the "necessary paperwork". It was apparent to all who met him that he clearly qualified for benefits. Yet months and months later, there was still no decision, no money, and no real help. At that point, he was told that unless an individual is homeless it takes well over a year to process a claim for benefits. A sad fact in America today is that the great bulk of our nation's homeless are indeed our former soldiers. Is that the way this generation wants to be remembered? Is America's greatest generation really those four generations ago whose accomplishments will never be equaled? Are we willing to accept that?

For a governmental agency to take a position that you must become destitute and homeless before expediting assistance is shameful. Hire more staff and get them working on fulfilling our promises. With billions of dollars of stimulus money being spent on far less worthwhile projects, we can and must do better. It is morally repre-

The Massachusetts School of Law
Veterans Association
Flag Pole Dedication

Life's Not Always a Day at the Beach

hensible to think a veteran must be homeless in the winter in New England or in the scorching heat of the South to get his file reviewed and acted upon in a timely manner. Lucky for our friend, he has friends who have friends whose voices are not as easily ignored. With the help of another serviceman, Senator John Kerry, the wheels of government bureaucracy moved a bit faster. However, Senator Kerry can't help everyone. America needs to help.

Instead of spending six billion dollars of stimulus money on various university building projects at Universities with bloated budges, shouldn't we do right by our men and women who are still bleeding in service of their country? President Obama, are you a man of your word?

Day 20 (Day +4)
Today is the day I would like to pull the blankets over my head until tomorrow. I miss my family, my dogs, my job, my life. I am fatigued, but will fight through it. I had zero cells for three days. Tomorrow will be a better day.

Day 21 (Day + 5)
Yesterday it really hit me. I was not feeling well – weak, fidgety, sick, restless, stir crazy, unable to settle; the medical team confirmed my cells were in the cellar and I needed to rest. Dr. Sanchorawala didn't want me walking up Massachusetts Avenue to the hospital (it's two blocks but feared I couldn't make it). There was a discussion of how I am doing exactly, and where I should be. Tomorrow I may need fluids and other medical necessities.

I was allowed to go back to the hotel after noon, and my mood lightened. Barreling into my room came a visit from my brother, to be followed by Whitey and Winnie, who looked great and were absolutely bonded to my sister and brother-in-law. I then learned Shadow was also living at my house.

Shadow is the old yellow Labrador retriever that Robert Burke rescued years ago. Mr. Burke, a Vietnam Veteran was going to be forced to quit his job so he could access his 401(k) retirement plan (his company did not permit current employees to access the account) to pay for surgery that Shadow needed, since he could not pay on his $488 weekly salary. Fortunately for Mr. Burke and Shadow, however, Mark E. Vogler of the Lawrence Eagle-Tribune wrote a story about Burke's predicament. The story attracted the attention of the Massachusetts School of Law and Dr. Richard Lindsay, founder of the Andover Animal Hospital. After examining Shadow, Dr. Lindsay agreed to perform the surgery if the law school could raise $1,000 to cover part of the cost. That was all I needed to hear, and I had my animal law class spread the word. People sent in so much money that there was a surplus after paying for the surgery. Thus, The Shadow Fund was established at the suggestion of Associate Dean, Michael L. Coyne, and Robert Burke to help pet owners who cannot afford necessary medical treatment for their pets. Shadow is now living with my sister and brother-in-law because Robert is dying of cancer.

Day 22 (Day + 6 through Day +12)
These were not easy days. Otherwise, my memory is a blur because I was too sick to write in my journal.

Day 23 (Day +13)
Dr. Sanchorawala gives me the green light to go home to sleep. So, I get to check out of the hotel. Each day, however, I am to go back to Boston Medical Center. I was not home six hours before the first crisis began;

Robert Burke and Shadow

Robert at Dodger Stadium,
Los Angles, CA

a large, hot, red lump in my right leg. Oh my God, I thought, I have a blood clot. I was also feeling terribly ill. I was up most of the night so we headed back to the hospital at 5:45 a.m. The medical team saw me right away. I told them I thought I had a blood clot. Dr. Sanchorawala arrived a few minutes later asking me how I learned to self-diagnoses a blood clot on myself, since I need cells for them to clot and I had no cells left! I told her, O.K., you look and tell me what it is. Within moments a shuttle service was called and I was on my way for an ultrasound. The good news, no blood clot; the bad news, a lump that they could not tell what it was! Infection? Cell rejection? Then what seemed like only moments later, the central line implanted in my chest started to also turn red. Dr. Sanchorawala said it had to come out. Dina was concerned about taking it out because my platelet count was too low. But, Dr. Sanchorawala won the discussion and I had every confidence I would not bleed to death. Removing the line in my neck was very difficult, and Dr. Sanchorawala joked that doing a heart transplant would be easier. We laughed our way through the ordeal without any bleeding incident.

Day 24 (Day +14) Happy Thanksgiving
Thankful to be alive even though I felt dead. It was great, though, to be home and have a day off from the hospital

Day 25 (Day +15)
Today, I was once again due back at Boston Medical first thing in the morning. So, my sister and I left at 5:45 a.m. Today, my visits were with Dr. Sloan, and Anthony, the nurse practitioner. Dr. Sloan had given me tremendous advice early in the process; that my job was to survive each day. He also said, "don't look ahead, only focus on that day." The next consideration for the

day: my inability to sleep. Anthony and Dr. Sloan made medication adjustments to try and help me sleep. I was going without sleep, save for 1½ hours, and that couldn't be good. Dr. Sloan said they would carefully monitor the lump in my leg, so I would be coming to the hospital next week.

Day 26 (Day +16)

I took the prescribed medicines to help me sleep, and although the combination of drugs helped me sleep, I felt "drugged" all day. I would not take these drugs again. It was uphill – the horrific side effects of aggressive chemo

Day 27 (Day +17)

I can barely walk upstairs. My body is depleted, I am very ill today. Food is an enemy, and drinking isn't much better.

Day 28 (Day +18)

I feel terrible. My blood pressure is 71/45 standing. I cannot stand longer than 90 seconds, or I will collapse. I begin to feel I will be unable to return to work, or even walk my dogs again. I am clearly not able to function. I am starting to lose hope in a return to MSL. I am fearful I will have to sell my house, because social security disability will not even cover my mortgage, and move back to Fitchburg where I am close to my family. I feel guilty that my sister is staying with me. She should be home with her husband and dog, not with me and my dogs, but she stays because she knows I am in bad shape. I cannot walk my dogs, drive to the hospital, or really do anything at all.

Day 29 (Day +19)

Dr. Sanchorawala made adjustments to my heart medicine in an effort to get my blood pressure up. I con-

Waiting for my appointment

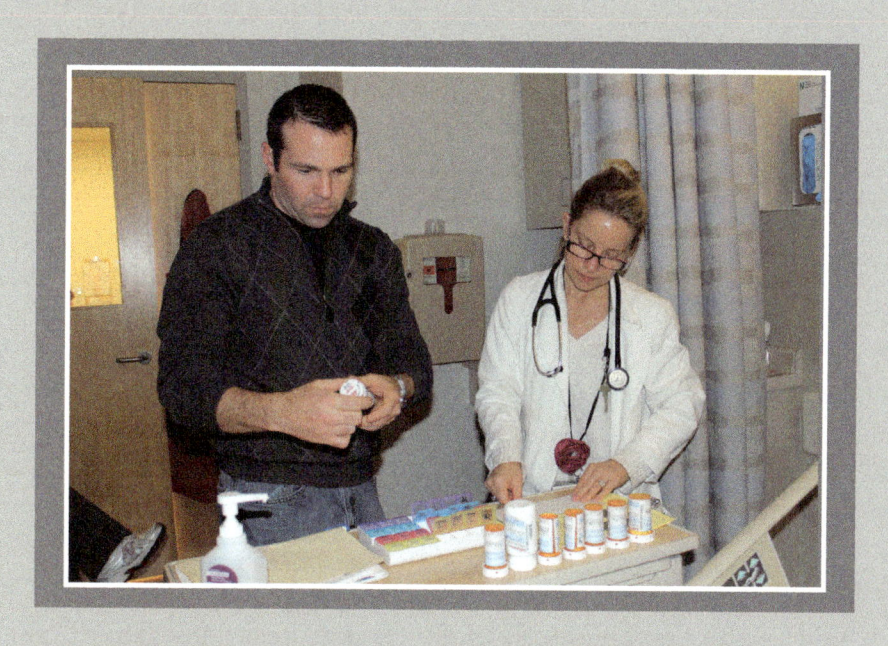

Michael and Dina setting up my pills

tinue to struggle. The 5:45 a.m. daily trip to Boston is getting to me. Am I ever going to get well enough to function? I do not like this.

Day 30 (Day +20)
Major improvement. My blood pressure is up. I feel better – not good, but better. I am still incredibly weak, but there are signs of improvement. Is this a fluke, or have I turned the corner?

Day 31 (Day +21)
I think I have turned the corner. I can now stand without feeling like I will collapse after ninety seconds. I walked my dogs with the help of my sister.

Day 32 (Day + 22)
Today is a great day! I am well enough to get discharged from the stem cell transplant unit. Beginning next week, my care shifts back to my Hematologist, Dr. Seldin; my primary doctor within the amyloid unit, Dr. O'Connell; and my primary care Doctor, Dr. Ingrid Hunt. I will remain medically compromised for one year. I plan to go back to work by mid-January, which if you look at me now, would require a miracle! My sister will pack up and return home tonight. Dr. Sanchorawala asked if I was strong enough to care for myself. I told her I was looking forward to taking care of myself. So, a warm goodbye from Dina, Dr. Sanchorawala, and my nurse, Cynthia.

Day 33 (Day +23)
I still barely sleep at night. I am wide awake in the early hours of the morning, ready to go (between 1:00 a.m. and 3:00 a.m., generally). Today is not an exception. I wake up at 3:00 a.m. and lay in bed until 5:00 a.m. This will be the first time I try and walk my dogs. Also, this

will be the first time I drive again. Clear the road, here I come! I put the dogs in the car and off we go. It was a successful morning (I did not bleed, hit the pavement, nor was I so fatigued that I could not finish). Christmas is in three weeks. Time to get some wreaths and the Christmas tree up.

Day 34 (Day +24)
Although the house is not fully decorated, the tree looks beautiful and that will suffice for this year. Normally, I enjoy transforming the entire house into a replica of the windows of the old Jordan Marsh, but that will have to wait until next year. For now, it is December 1st, I am alive and doing fine!

Day 35 (Day +33)
My visit with Dr. Seldin went well. I am doing well and we discussed my return to work in mid-January. He asked me how I planned to prevent infections and getting germs. We settled on the four foot rule - - keeping a distance of four feet from persons, and no interactions with ill students. Dr. Seldin was also concerned about Christmas, so we discussed safe procedures for a limited family gathering. As it was, I had a cold, so antibiotics were in order.

40 DAYS
I am forty days post transplant, and with Christmas less than a week away, I thought it is time to evaluate where I am physically. Each day is a better day with minor set backs along the long road to recovery. During the weeks when my blood pressure was 71/45 standing, I was starting to give up hope. Unable to stand for longer than ninety seconds, I worried I would never be able to walk my dogs again. The thought of returning to work, and the law school I love, no longer seemed to be a reality. If

Life's Not Always a Day at the Beach

I couldn't stand, and was too weak to function, how would I ever stand at a podium and teach a class? I was starting to think the life I loved was over. I began to wonder if I would have to sell my home. Where would I go? What would happen to my dogs and me? What would I do?

I did not give up hope, but it was difficult to stay positive. I needed 24 hour care, and walking up a flight of stairs was harder than running a marathon. I had to sit and rest after just three steps. My sister had to stay with me for weeks, leaving her family at home. I felt like a dependent toddler.

I have always loved Christmas. I decorate the whole house, inside and out, and my family gathers at my house to celebrate life, each other, and the holiday. Somehow, I got the tree up and decorated it, but no other decorations this year, except what Nancy managed to do outside. It usually takes me thirty hours to decorate and I simply do not now have the strength to do that. Because my immune system is compromised for one year, I cannot interact with kids – and any potential risk of illness or infection from adults precludes my typical celebration and festivities.

Although my blood pressure remains low, so low that sometimes the machine can't read it, I am overall regaining my strength and doing well. I no longer visit the medical center daily, and Nancy has returned to her home, although she never leaves me alone long. I feel some sense of independence, and returning to work in the middle of January on a reduced teaching load, is now a more realistic goal. Although I always planned to be back for the start of the semester, this is the first week I feel I can actually do it.

Finally, I am able to walk my dogs. Although I remain weak, I continue to get stronger. The dogs and I pick easy walks, but yesterday we took the hill.

I feel lucky. I am progressing. I know for many stem cell transplant patients to recover it takes a full year to fight the extraordinary fatigue.

It takes six months to determine if the stem cell patient is in remission. I have a scheduled appointment in February: I suspect to take an early look at my light chains to see if remission is on the horizon. My focus is on restoring my strength and health, and I will worry about remission later. I return to Boston Medical the week of July 4th for the verdict.

The MSL Leaf Crew
Tyrone, Mick, Mary, Jerry, Joe, Jeannie, Mike, John, Pam and Dan

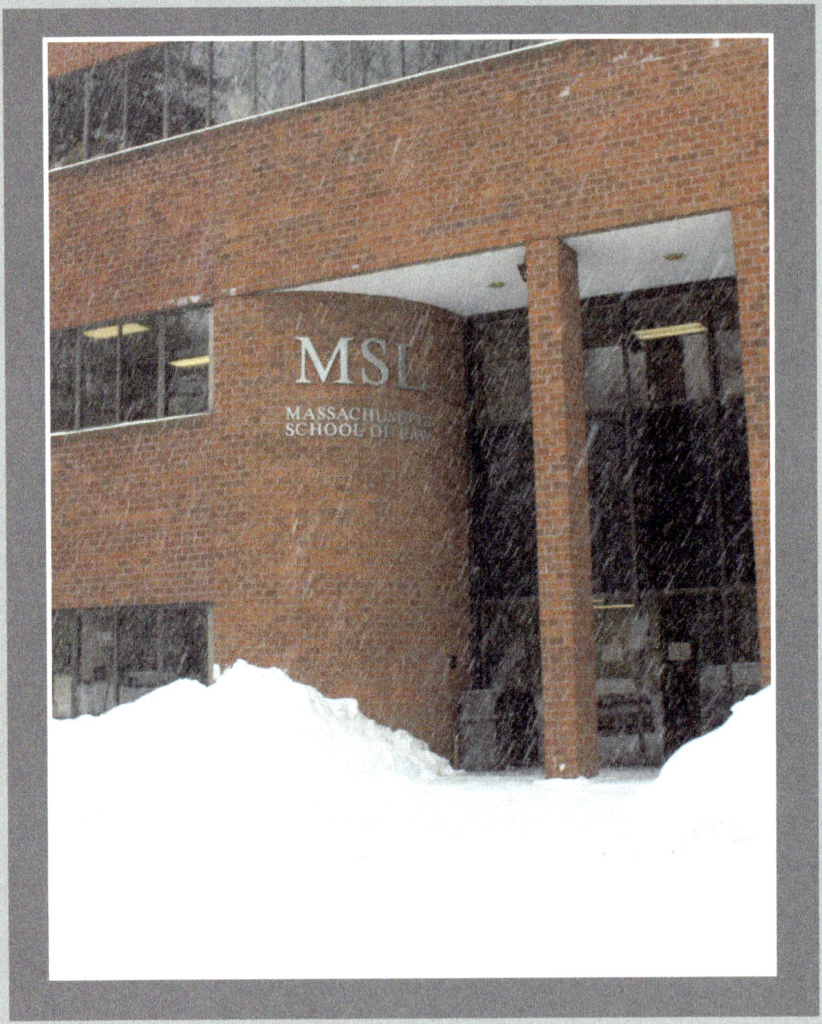
MSL

THE BLIZZARD OF 2013

A massive blizzard was scheduled to hit Massachusetts on Friday, bringing two to three feet of snow. The law school, and nearly all educational institutions and businesses were closed; so I was surprised when Dr. O'Connell called to discuss my recent lab results and the medical team's conclusions.

The news wasn't great - - although there was some improvement in my light chains, it was not the significant decrease that was hoped for. However, these results are early (three months from the stem cell transplant) and a final result will not be reached until six months from the transplant. Accordingly, we will all hope for improvement and Dr. O'Connell rescheduled a comprehensive follow-up, including a bone marrow biopsy, for May 8th (yuk). A bone marrow biopsy is done to evaluate whether the disease is in the bone marrow – the tissue inside the bones.

It is a painful procedure and the skill level of the doctor taking the biopsy determines how bad the pain will be. Patients really fear the procedure and I am no exception. I have seen patients faint from the apprehension and some get up and walk out of the hospital when their name is called. I asked what would be next, if the results were not favorable - - perhaps a different chemotherapy, depending on what the bone biopsy shows? While the news was disappointing, it was still too soon on the timeline for me to worry, so I decided, after I shared the results with a few close people, it would be best to forget about it for now. After all, I am feeling pretty good.

The significant snowfall was a dose of reality, however. Mike Coyne had arranged plowing for me as a Christmas gift, and if he had not I probably would still be buried inside. Shoveling was something I had always enjoyed, but now I found myself struggling to clear paths for the dogs. I found myself saying, the old Diane could do this no problem – but this Diane cannot.

A few days later, the snow was the least of my problems because the snow turned to ice that I didn't see, so I ended up back in Boston Medical with a broken shoulder. Now, what was it I said about living alone? When the hospital thought I should go to a rehab facility, I decided to go home, again dependent on my sister, who once again had returned to my house to care for my dogs while I was hospitalized. She agreed to stay and help me, but I doubt she realized what this would entail. I was totally dependent on her; I couldn't get dressed, remove the cover of my pill bottles, or do even the most basic tasks without help.

THE BLIZZARD OF 2013

Tommy Kirk and Fess Parker from the Walt Disney film *Old Yeller*

"That was rough . . . Thing to do now is try and forget it . . . I guess I don't quite mean that. It's not anything you can forget. Maybe not even a thing you want to forget . . . Life's like that sometimes . . . Now and then for no good reason a man can figure out, life will just haul off and knock him flat, slam him agin' the ground so hard it seems like all his insides is busted. But it's not all like that. A lot of it's mighty fine, and you can't afford to waste the good part frettin' about the bad. That makes it bad . . . Sure, I know – sayin' it's one thing and feelin' it's another. But I'll tell you a trick that's sometimes a big help. When you start lookin' around for something good to take the place of the bad, as a general rule you can find it."

                             From the movie *Old Yeller*

25th Anniversary Pre-Graduation Party

Rosa Colon at Law Day

Receiving The Bell Award at Law Day

MSLAW Police Chiefs honored at Law Day

SIX MONTHS LATER

We sleep soundly in our beds because rough men stand ready in the night to visit violence on those who would do us harm.
                                        Winston Churchill

Saturday was Law Day, and the day's festivities started with a faculty meeting with MSL's Board of Trustees who had flown in for a meeting and the evening's Law Day Gala, which in part was a celebration of the school's 25th year anniversary. We recognized our three founding trustees, as well as six of the ten Massachusetts School of Law graduates who have gone on to become Chief of Police. It was wonderful to see all of them and celebrate their accomplishments. In light of the bombings at the Boston Marathon three weeks earlier and the recognition of the sacrifice police make for all our safety and the tremendous job they did in apprehending the bombers,

MSLAW Trustees

Paula, Beverly Chorbajian, Mike and I

Mike, Eugene O'Flaherty, Larry and I

SIX MONTHS LATER

our appreciation for their service runs deep. Also, one of our own alumns, Beverly Chorbajian, a dedicated civil rights and criminal defense attorney, was the recipient of the Thurgood Marshall Award and our key note speaker. Rosa Colon received the Dean's Award for achievement, completing a fourteen year journey to graduate from MSL. Rosa had been involved in a near fatal car accident that left her a quadriplegic. Tonight we all celebrated her remarkable achievement in completing law school. So it was a wonderful, albeit a late evening for me. I was recognized by the students and Mike Coyne and that was nice because it gave me a chance to thank them all for the privilege of teaching at MSL. It has been a wonderful period in my life.

Sunday was a prep day for my upcoming two day return to Boston Medical Center for my re-evaluation of the success of the stem cell transplant. My eyelids have been bruising and bleeding significantly recently, so I am not really sure that I will receive the news I am hoping for: complete favorable response = durable remission. Since my very preliminary tests taken months ago showed some improvement, but not enough improvement, I am hopeful this upcoming visit will produce results sufficient to indicate I will live at least long enough to outlive my dogs, and see my two eldest nephews finish their education. Anything more than that would be a wonderful gift, anything short of that, a heartbreak for me.

Kathy Villare picked me up early for the trip into Boston Medical. She had some television taping to do, so she offered to drive me. I was excited to go hoping ultimately for positive news, but dreading the necessary bone marrow biopsy. Two key indicators would be: my light chain number hoping the stem cell transplant reduced the light chains to normal ranges as a high level of free light chains is not consistent with a favorable outcome. Also, the bone marrow biopsy was critical to whether the transplant and chemotherapy brought the number down from 25% of my bones still manufacturing this disease. If only you didn't need a bone marrow biopsy to determine this because the process is so painful. The first time I thought I would go into shock afterwards. I remember standing outside the hospital sobbing uncontrollably with passerbys stopping. It was awful. The second time wasn't so bad and I think the doctor conducting the procedure makes all the difference. Dr. Seldin did my second bone marrow, and like everything else he does, he was superb. Unlike the first time, I had little pain afterwards.

When I was called in for the bone marrow, I felt my knees grow weak. The procedure was done by a young, foreign fellow who announced she was very good at it, but didn't want to jinx herself so would say no more. She asked me to drop my waistline and lie face down on the bed. Oh God how I dreaded this. I become her co-pilot telling her what was key was a lot of numbing medicine deep (that's what Dr. Seldin told the doctor with him when he did my last one). She said, "Yes, that's correct". So wonder she didn't slug me! The procedure was painful but quick, and not bad, all things considered. The doctor regulated my breathing like I was in childbirth and it helped. When I exited the procedure room into the waiting area, three other patients stood up quickly and shouted, "How was it?" I asked them whether they were awaiting a bone marrow and in unison they said, "Yes, how bad was it? they echoed. "Not bad at all," I responded. One of them piped up, "Did you take the ativan?" I immediately thought, I didn't know that was an option; if I had known, I would have taken a bottle.

I thought I would calm them by telling them this

SIX MONTHS LATER

was my third bone marrow biopsy and the doctor was very good – had done 200 bone marrow biopsies to date. One patient said this would be her third and her second was very bad. She fled the hospital the last time they called her name to come in. We all discussed what a difference it makes as to the skill of the doctor and I assured them this one was terrific (an overstatement).

The rest of the day was testing and fact finding, with some results expected the next day, but the crucial bone marrow biopsy results would not be in till Friday. Accordingly, I had a few tests left the next day, and then I would meet individually with Doctors O'Connell and Seldin. My light chains number should be available and that is a key marker in my response to the stem cell transplant.

By the time I was heading home from the first day's evaluation, the numbing medication from the bone marrow biopsy was wearing off and the pain was setting in. The night would follow with a lot of pain, several heating pads, and a lot of sleepless hours.

Day Two at Boston Medical included an echocardiogram and meetings with my favorite pair, Doctors Seldin and O'Connell. The news was good, but not terrific: preliminary test showed the stem cell process had a very successful impact on my kidneys. The total protein from my kidneys was so low it could not be calculated because it was below measurable range. Yeah! Likewise, my heart was much improved. The news was not as positive for my liver results, but the real key number is the serum free light chains which were greatly improved, but not enough to free me from further treatment (oh no – more chemo). Although a final decision on future treatment plans awaits my bone biopsy results due at week's end, to quote

Off to ref football! Just kidding, that's my outfit for a women's tackle football show.

SIX MONTHS LATER

Dr. Seldin, "Don't worry. I have more tricks up my sleeve . . . enjoy the summer . . . don't only work. . . do some fun things".

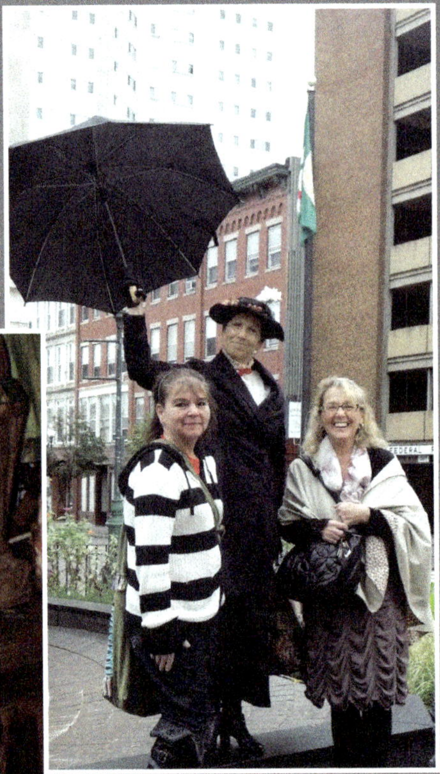

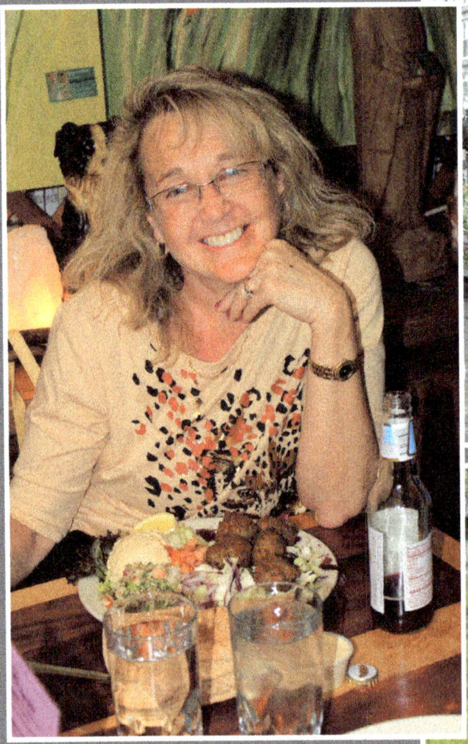

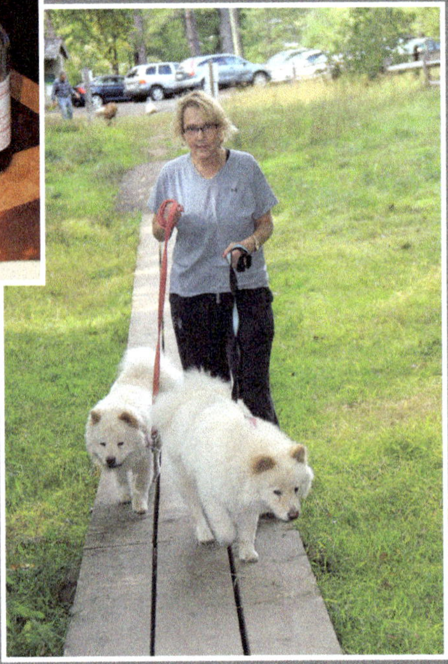

LESSONS LEARNED FROM THE STEM CELL TRANSPLANT

1. Get up early and always make your bed. Otherwise, you might be tempted to stay there!
2. Be tough, at least tougher than what happens to you
3. Don't stay down, get yourself back up
4. No self-pity, others have it worse
5. Hold onto hope
6. Accept that life may not be easy
7. Laugh as much as possible
8. Family and friends are everything
9. Be kind
10. Find inner strength when you need it
11. View the process as a worthwhile one in your life
12. Don't worry
13. Treat yourself well
14. Let go of grudges
15. Always stay positive
16. Keep working! Being productive is good for the soul

Senator George G. Vest
Missouri

EPILOGUE

"The best friend a man has in the world may turn against him and become his enemy. His son or daughter that he has reared with loving care may prove ungrateful. Those who are nearest and dearest to us, those whom we trust with our happiness and good name, may become traitors to their faith.

"The money that a man has he may lose. It flies away from him, perhaps when he needs it most. A man's reputation may be sacrificed in a moment of ill-considered action.

"The people who are prone to fall on their knees to do us honor when success is with us may be the first to throw the stone of malice when failure settles its cloud upon our heads.

Life's Not Always a Day at the Beach

"The one absolutely unselfish friend that a man can have in this selfish world, the one that never deserts him, the one that never proves ungrateful or treacherous, is his dog.

"Gentlemen of the jury, a man's dog stands by him, in prosperity and poverty, in health and sickness. He will sleep on the cold ground, where the winter wind blows and the snow drives fiercely if only he may be near his master's side. He will kiss the hand that has no food to offer; he will lick the wounds and sores that come in encounter with the roughness of the world. He guards the sleep of his pauper master as if he were a prince.

"When all other friends desert, he remains. When riches take wing and reputation falls to pieces, he is as constant in his love as the sun in its journey through the heavens. "If fortune drives his master for the an outcast in the world, friendless and homeless, the faithful dog asks no higher privilege than that of accompanying him to guard against danger, to fight his enemies, and when the last scene of all comes and death takes the master in its embrace and his body is laid away, there by his graveside will the noble dog be found, his head between his paws, his eyes sad but open in alert watchfulness, faithful and true even unto death."

The memorable words of the late Senator George G. Vest of Missouri as a young lawyer.

****

EPILOGUE

When I woke up that Friday morning and saw that it was already light outside, I knew something was wrong - - it was after 5:00 a.m. and my dogs simply laid sleeping. This past week Whitey was refusing to walk, and now this morning he refused to eat - - a very first for Whitey. It was time to call our veterinarian. My sense was Whitey was dying. I did not like that hollow look in his eyes, the same look I had seen in mom, then dad, and then Hakuna.

By the time Dr. Letwin took Whitey from me to do bloodwork and an ultrasound, I was sobbing because I knew the results would not be good. Dr. Letwin confirmed my fears, Whitey had malignant tumors, and was anemic from internal bleeding, and there was nothing she could do to save him. She sent Whitey home with me telling me to bring him back to be put to sleep whenever he would tell me to do so.

Whitey held on - - quiet and comfortable - -Not interested in walking or eating - - unless it's his favorite donut or Danish. Each day I thought was his last, but his tail still wagged and he looked at me as if to say, "one more day, one more donut, and just let me rest please."

Winnie knew what was happening. She kissed his forehead. I don't know which surprised me most, that she did this kind gesture, or that Whitey allowed it. Either way, it brought comfort to the three of us.

My bone marrow biopsy showed some decrease of amyloids in my bones, but not enough. I will return to Boston Medical Center for a reevaluation in three months and a new course of treatment to continue this fight for a healthy tomorrow.

Winnie, Whitey and Me

EPILOGUE

Until then, three months of no treatment is a gift for me to enjoy each sunrise. I will use the time to teach and regain my strength for the next round that awaits.

Michael, Chrissy, Colin and Aidan

APPENDIX

And in the end it's not the years in your life that count. It's the life in your years.
Abraham Lincoln

My Brother's Journal

October 16, 2012
First entry: All is well with a week to go. Diane starts her treatment next Wednesday. I will keep everyone updated with posts and pictures as often as I can.

October 24, 2012
We just arrived at Boston Medical for day 1. Diane is in great spirits and we are ready to take this thing on! Thanks to everyone for your outcries of love and support. It means the world to Di. More to come soon.

October 24th Part 2
Well we are home for the night and it was a great first

Life's Not Always a Day at the Beach

---

day. We received a lot of information and Diane had a lot of tests done. She did great!! A funny story to share is that I had to wear a mask today. I am super protective and cautious and decided it would be a good idea. Well as we were in the waiting room and I was looking through my backpack and moving around, I took down my mask and was sweating pretty good. Diane looks over and starts laughing at me. She says, "People are going to think you are getting ready to blow the place up." Maybe you had to be there, but I am still laughing as I type this post!! We ended the day at one of Diane's favorite places for a frozen yogurt!!

October 25th
Today Diane came in for the placement of her catheter port. This is needed for collection and administration of stem cells and chemotherapy. It was an early day and Diane just came out of surgery. She is in a little uncomfortable, but overall is doing well and is in recovery. We hope to head home in the next few hours to walk the dogs!!

October 26th
Diane had another great day today. It was a real testament to her strength. She woke up this morning full of energy and ready to go. This was amazing after the long day she had yesterday. I failed to mention that she went into A-fib yesterday during surgery. She is fine, but that added to the long day. Today was another long day, but not quite as physically demanding. She had blood work and a lot of labs, they cleaned the ports and then finally ended the day with the growth factor injections. In short, the goal of these injections is to grow as many additional stem cells as possible. Starting next week they will be extracting and collecting her stem cells to be given back to her after the chemotherapy. The rest of the weekend entails additional growth factor shots, so she is home in

APPENDIX

bed asleep for the night. At the end of the first few days, things are going very well!!

October 27th
As we move along here Diane remains a trooper as we all expected. She remains upbeat and positive. Last night was a little rough as she experienced a lot of pain in her bones. This is to be expected as the growth factor injections essentially cause this. As I mentioned earlier the growth factor injections are given to help her create more stem cells, many more in fact. The result is that it essentially forces the bones to expand which cause a lot of pain. Diane went in again today for another one of these shots and will get a third shot tomorrow. Otherwise the week should be pretty quiet, with as much sleeping as possible. Diane hopes to watch the Notre Dame game tonight, but we will see about that. She is lucky I love ND as much as she does, but I hope we sleep through the game to find out they won tomorrow!! Have a great night everyone and I will report back again tomorrow. Below is a quick picture of Diane relaxing at the hospital yesterday :)

October 28th
It has been a tough couple of days for Diane. She is experiencing a lot of bone pain. She has been a real trooper and they have finally given her some additional pain medication. There is not a lot that she can take, but she has been able to dull the pain a little. The good news is that as always Diane remains positive and continues to look forward. Tomorrow is the first of the stem cell collection days. We have another early morning in Boston, but I will keep you updated with the progress.

October 29th
Diane had a little bit rougher day today. She was sick most of the day as a result of the treatments, but got

Life's Not Always a Day at the Beach

through it. The good news is that they were able to collect a lot of stem cells. This is essential and they were very happy about it. The other great news is that the care here is unbelievable. Diane had 3 doctors working on her care most all of the day. There were multiple nurses and the transplant coordinator overseeing her as well. In the end, she made it through a rough day and still remains really positive. She said to me last night with a big laugh, "Well Michael, they didn't kill me." She is feeling better and ready for tomorrow!!!

October 30th
Just a quick update. Diane is feeling a bit better today. She has eaten and doing better. I just thought everyone would want to know that!! I will relay the notes of the day later tonight.

October 31st
Happy Halloween. Great news. Diane is feeling much better and says that she is doing great. Spending the morning here at Boston Medical today, but as of right now she will have tomorrow off!! The stem cell collection went well in terms of numbers collected. All in all, I can report that Diane looks great and is feeling great and most importantly the treatment is going great. On a related note, for anyone that is getting the Michael as Batman stories on Halloween, don't believe everything that you hear from my sister :)

She is now home in Andover enjoying a frozen yogurt, Dr.'s orders.

November 2nd
Yesterday was a well deserved off day and went just fine. Today we were back in the clinic for a series of tests and meetings about the upcoming treatments scheduled for

APPENDIX

next week. In short, the day went very well!! Diane's numbers are great and she is in great shape to take on the chemotherapy which starts Monday morning. It will be a long day Monday, but I will update you all when I get a minute.

Also, Diane was really moved when we arrived home to find the good luck banner and pictures. Your support means the world to her and to me as well. Diane is lucky to have such amazing people in her life and we are all very lucky to have here as well. So have a great weekend and go ND.

November 5th
We moved Diane into the hotel at Boston last night and that went pretty well. We made our way over to CVS to pick up her 9 prescriptions! Today was the beginning of the chemotherapy. It involved an hour ice treatment of keeping ice in her mouth to prevent sores from the treatment. This was a real challenge for Diane, but she made it through like a trooper! It is 5:00 and we are back at the hotel resting. She is doing very well. We repeat the same process again tomorrow.

November 6th
Well the good news is that day 2 of the ice treatments are officially done. I am writing from Diane's bedside today. It really was a bad process for her, but she handled it very well. Whether we have referred to it as a version of water torture, but neither Diane, Kathy or I would make good spies!! From here tomorrow and Thursday are relatively easy days in terms of the treatments themselves. Tomorrow is a blood draw and check-up while Thursday is the infusion of her cells. That will be long but not too bad. The bad news is that Diane will start to become sick from the chemotherapy and treatments. It is likely that she

Life's Not Always a Day at the Beach

will be hospitalized over the next couple weeks so please do not be alarmed if that makes the posts. It is a tough road head but all is going as well as we can hope for! As soon as we are cleared to leave for the day, Diane will be headed home as the key for the next few days is sleep and recovery. Di sends her love to everyone and thanks you all for your support.

November 7th
Diane had a rough start to her day today. She went to her appointment at the clinic today and they have her back on track. Good news is that she is back at the hotel doing well and is actually getting much needed sleep. Tomorrow is another big day. Diane will be getting an infusion of her stem cells. This means that she will be getting her stem cells back. In the next day or two, her system will crash a bit as her white blood cells will be essentially at 0. This is considered day 0. The impact of chemo will start to kick in and she will likely be tired and sick. However this is the plan. It is not fun, but it is what is needed to come out on the other side!! She remains ever positive and ready for the challenge. As you all know, that is her way. She is an amazing woman and has shown this again. Her grace through all of this is truly amazing!! Have a great night and I will report back tomorrow.

November 8th
Sorry for the delay in posting this update. Diane did great today. It went as well as it could have! It was a long day. The process today was about 8 hours or so. It was prep work, 2 hours of hydration, the stem cell infusion and then 2 more hours of hydration. As I said it all went very well. I can't say again how great the team is. Diane had 4 doctors in the room for the better part of the day. It was 4 of the most brilliant woman you could imagine, well 5 with Diane. Now comes the hard part. The

APPENDIX

next couple weeks will be her body reacting to the chemo and treatments. She will likely start to get sick early next week and it expected to last at least a couple of weeks. From here she will slowly begin to recover. The goal is to be out of the hotel in 3 weeks, but we will not know if she is in remission for 6 months. A lot of information for one day, but I promised to keep everyone informed.
He is a picture of Di's meds. One of the doctors and I setting up her pill box for the week. Nine meds multiple times a day. Crazy!!!! Again, all is well at this time. Di is headed home to rest

November 10th
Diane remains pretty steady. Her weight and blood counts remain the same and she has been doing a lot of walking. Overall she is doing great. A slight decrease in energy levels, but that is what was expected. Not a lot to report in terms of changes or new information. We are in the calm before the storm here, but as I mentioned she will crash a bit, so do not be too alarmed. She is doing great!

November 12th
Diane had a scheduled visit for blood work today and it confirmed that her counts had dropped pretty significantly, which was expected to happen. Ironically she felt better today than yesterday and was able to eat a bit. She had a visit from the dogs today as well and that seemed to raise her spirits. All in all, she is still doing very well. As I mentioned before the next week to 10 days or more will be tough. I'll keep everyone posted. She loves you all.

November 13th
Today was another day at the clinic for hydration and blood draws. We learned today that her white cells were at 0, so now we wait as her body recovers. Diane is tired,

but considering the stage of the treatment, they thought she was doing great. She is on a treatment of rest and plenty of drinking right now (no fun drinks!!). So a hard week or so ahead, but Diane is doing great all things considered.

Also, thanks to all the folks from MSL that raked the yard today. That is a huge help and relief for our family!! You guys are great!!!!!

November 14th
Another Day in the books and Diane is still doing well. She received a couple bags of platelets today as her counts are low. Again, this was to be expected, so nothing out of the norm here. Biggest issue for Diane is that she is very fatigued. She is still pushing herself to make the walk from the hotel to the hospital each day, but she might need to back off of that for a couple days as a preventive measure. Her counts are so low that it would not be good if she fell or something along those lines. That is about the biggest news of the day. In short, Diane is tired and depleted, but overall she is really doing very well. She continues to show just how strong she is and why we all know that she will beat this!!

November 16th
Diane is having a pretty rough day. She is experiencing extreme fatigue and is really just sleeping a lot. We have convinced her to get a ride to and from the hospital, so that is going fine and removes any risk of an accidental fall. Today, she is at the hospital receiving platelets and fluids. The great news is that her white blood cells are rising and that means that she is producing them which is great news!! The fatigue is expected as part of this period, so essentially Diane is on track and doing well. Just a rough period for her.

APPENDIX

November 19th
Good news is that according to the Dr.'s, Diane is doing great!! She continues to have some rough days, but her white counts continue to rise and overall she is doing well. Today she will be in the hospital most of the day receiving fluids and platelets. She is very fatigued and ravaged by the treatment, but again she is doing very well. The team will be meeting tomorrow with more of an update on where Diane is and what the next weeks will look like. On a side note: Diane would like to remind everyone that the Fighting Irish are #1 in the country. Very fitting!!

November 20th
I just spoke with the head of Diane's team. In what I can only consider amazing news, Diane will be heading home by Thanksgiving!! Now, that does not mean that she is out of the woods, but she is doing very well. She will still be going in and out of Boston for the rest of this week and next week, but she has been doing amazing. On the days they were expecting to see side effects at their worst, she looked amazing. Having said that, she is still experiencing what they call delayed side effects including extreme fatigue!! So she will not be up for visitors or anything of that nature, but I know being home with her dogs should be a real boost for her. Our family will still be staying with Diane 24/7, so she is in good hands (well, I guess I have to say that :)). All kidding aside, this is a great day. Diane is the fastest release in the program's history. Living in Andover helps her early release, but still wildly impressive. They expect her to be "dismissed" from this stage of the program by the end of next week. Still, it can take people over a year to recover from this treatment. I can't tell you what Diane has been through, but she is a real warrior. Happy early Thanksgiving to you all!! We are certainly thankful around these parts!!!

Life's Not Always a Day at the Beach

November 21st
Well as some of you know, it has been a real roller-coaster ride since Diane was released. She has been back at the hospital since early this morning as she has endured some major complications. She will be given a couple new medications and hopefully will sleep the next day or two. In the end, she will be headed back home again, but is still in a real fight here. I will keep everyone posted, but she will likely be out of commission for a few days. Do keep Di in your thoughts as she still has a long road ahead, but she sends her love to everyone.

November 26th
Sorry that it has been soling since I updated the page. I wanted to let folks know that Diane is still doing well. It has been a bit of a roller coaster in that Di has her ups and downs. As was expected she is still exhausted just about all the time. She has been able to stay at home and make trips in to the clinic. She spent the better part of the day there today receiving fluids and being monitored. They do a wonderful job there and she is in great hands. Also, she remains ever positive and continues to fight! Please know that she misses you all and send her love. I pass along the messages from everyone and I know it warms her heart. I thank you all for your thoughts and well wishes for Diane.

December 3rd
Just a quick update. Diane is starting to get a little of her energy back. The team has made adjustments to her medicines and she is doing a lot better. By no means is she back to normal as she is still under house confinement, but I wanted people to know that she is starting to feel better. Last week was a long, hard week for her. Thus, this is very positive. Also, she is no longer going in and out of the stem cell transplant clinic every day. She

APPENDIX

will still go to Boston a couple times a week and the team will be in close and constant contact, but this too is positive news!!

December 20th
Sorry for the lack of recent posts, but the reason is that Diane continues to make slow, but steady steps in her recovery. She is working to regain her strength for a return to MSL for the January semester!! Diane and our family thank you all so very much for the thoughts, prayers and continued support!! Happy Holidays to all. Spend time with your loved ones and enjoy this time.

Whipped to the Finish and Dead on the Track
By Diane Sullivan & Holly Vietzke

Romance. Grace. Sport. Horse racing has a rich tradition in our country. As we watch this "Sport of Kings" on television, we are treated to images of women in extravagant hats and garb, men in splendid tailored suits, and children lovingly coiffed and attired. And then we gaze upon the beautiful, powerful horses - athletic, prancing, waiting to charge toward the finish line - - aiming to please, aiming to win. How exciting it appears to all of us.

Not really. It's an illusion - - It's a fraud – And, too often, this romanticized image dissolves into animal cruelty and death. Eight Belles was killed on the track at last week's Kentucky Derby. Barbaro fractured three bones in his ankle in the 2006 Preakness Stakes and was killed eight months later. And don't forget 2005 Horse of the Year, Saint Liam, who broke his left leg while backing away from his handlers. He was killed, as well. His funeral expenses were fully covered, for he had earned his owners more than 4 million dollars.

Those of us who teach animal law tell our students that societal attitude toward animals has changed. We tell them the status of animals is marked by companion and humaneness, and our laws reflect that new status. Except in horse racing. The images and pictures from the Kentucky Derby are unbearable. And so is the benighted and sentimental quote from Eight Belles' trainer, Larry Jones: "We put everything into them that we have, and they give us everything they have. They put their lives on the line, and *she was glad to do it.*" This is nonsense.

One hundred and sixty years after the passage of our states' first anti-cruelty law, which was enacted in response to a horse race that ended with both horses dropping dead, we feel as if we're in a time warp.

APPENDIX

The question then is, why? Where did our compassion for horses go? Too often we read and hear about the abuses in the horse racing industry, all done in the name of amusement and economic pursuit. Anyone who watched the Derby should now recognize that animals are sentient creatures capable of experiencing great pain. With this recognition must come change.

We must start to investigate these injuries as animal cruelty cases. How many more Eight Belles, Barbaros, and Saint Liams must there be before we take action to stop these deaths?

Aficionados of horse racing refute the allegations of cruelty by saying that these horses are coddled, well cared for, and live in luxury. Well, many horse owners who do not race their beloved animals also coddle and care for them very well—often times putting their own needs second to those of the horses. A friend of one of us has a mother who has horses in Colorado. Every Independence Day and New Year's Eve, she stays outside all night to calm the horses when the fireworks go off. And when she feeds them their carrots, she eats with them, so as to keep them company. She even rescued a horse that could not be ridden just so all the horses could have more "friends." Those horses may not be fed the most expensive meals or given the highest quality bedding, but they are probably a lot happier being able to walk around in the pasture at their leisure than if they were confined to a stable and whipped when ridden.

And what good is living in luxury if, at the tender age of three, the horse is no longer living at all? The deaths that make the news—such as those of Eight Belles and Barbaro—do so only because they occur during one of the Triple Crown races, to high-profile thoroughbreds. But how many other horses at smaller tracks around the country also die that we don't hear about? A 2001 article reported that in North America, approximately 800 horses per year die due to racing injuries.[1] That number is likely even higher today, with the prevalence of steroids and other drugs pumped into

---

1   Miller, Ted, *Six Recent Horse Deaths at Emerald Downs Spark Concern,* Seattle Post-Intelligencer, May 8, 2001.

Life's Not Always a Day at the Beach

the thoroughbreds. In the summer of 2006, there were 19 deaths at one race track alone.[2] And those are just the deaths: *Washington Post* columnist Sally Jenkins reported that on average, *two horses per day* suffer career-ending injuries.[3] For an animal that loves to run (another pro-racing argument), this is hardly a life of luxury.

Proponents also claim that horse racing is a sport, exhibiting grace and pure athleticism at its finest, and as with any sport, injuries occur. But the difference here is that these "athletes" are not willing participants, assuming the risk of injury as human athletes do. Add to that the fact that their injuries often result in death, and the analogy isn't even close.

When it comes to determining whether a particular practice constitutes animal cruelty, courts may allow the practice if there is a legitimate or religious purpose for it. Unless one considers gambling a legitimate purpose, horse racing seemingly has none. These horses are bred for the sole purpose of racing and making many people much money. And once they have served that purpose, they are bred to other horses to produce offspring that will generate more money. If gambling on horses were illegal, would horse racing even exist?

So what should be done? Outlaw horse racing or prosecute it like other cases of animal cruelty? At a minimum, there should be no more whipping and no more forced entry into the gate. That is animal cruelty. Whipping a horse forces it to run through pain, and in Eight Belles' case, until she had no legs left to stand on. And when a horse doesn't want to go into the gate, do not force it to do so. Scratch the horse from the race. Another minimal step would be to change the track surfaces to synthetic surfaces, which causes fewer injuries.

Cruelty to Animals in Massachusetts is defined as "whoever over-

---

2 Arrington, Debbie, *Synthetic horse tracks called safer but slower*, Sacramento Bee, p A1, April 21, 2007.

3 Jenkins, Sally, *Is Horse Racing Breeding Itself to Death?* Wash. Post p. D01, May 4, 2008.

APPENDIX

works...cruelly beat(s)... and whoever uses in a cruel or inhumane manner in a race, game, or contest . . . or permits it to be subjected to unnecessary torture, suffering or cruelty of any kind...."

The romance and grace of horse racing is illusory. The deaths are real.

Diane Sullivan and Holly Vietzke are professors of law at the Massachusetts School of Law at Andover and teach the school's animal law course.

TIME TO HUNT DOWN TIGER ABUSE
By Diane Sullivan, Holly Vietzke, and Rose Church
Massachusetts School of Law

Parents in Massachusetts bring their children to the zoo to see tigers. Parents in Maine need only bring them to their neighbor's house, where it is legal to keep a tiger as a pet. In fact, the Bangor city code prohibits a resident from having more than three dogs as pets, but a tiger—or any wild animal—is perfectly fine.

States regulate the keeping of tigers within state lines, and the laws vary state to state. Today, 21 states allow private citizens to acquire or keep a tiger as a pet with as little a requirement as a license or permit (and some do not even require that). In fact, more tigers live within the United States than in the rest of the world, although the total number is speculation since there are no tracking or monitoring regulations in place. The state of Texas alone has more tigers (more than 2,000) than all of India (1,700).

One reason for the preponderance of tiger-owners is the increasing number of cub-petting displays in malls which, under practices established by the U.S. Department of Agriculture (USDA), is legal when a tiger is eight to twelve weeks old. Aside from the cruelty and abuse this represents for the tigers, exhibitors line their pockets as they send the wrong message that these cute, wild animals can be kept as pets. The private keeping of wild, exotic animals as domestic pets generally leads to the animal being kept in horrible, deplorable conditions, risking harm to both the tiger and the public. In fact, thousands of tigers are living in abysmal conditions in cages, often owned by people who buy them on a whim.

And what happens to these cubs—which were bred for this sole, profitable purpose—after 12 weeks? More than likely, the cub ends up spending its life in a small concrete cage, or is sold for its "parts." It may even end up in your local butcher shop—hardly

APPENDIX

a fair fate for such a noble beast.

In 2003, upon tips from tenants, police discovered and removed a Bengal tiger living in an apartment in Harlem. Although owning tigers is illegal in New York, police suspect that the tiger was purchased legally elsewhere as a cub and brought to the city. This is precisely why a federal ban is necessary. Yet the federal government has actually made it *easier* to own a tiger when, in 1998, the U.S. Fish and Wildlife Service lifted the licensing requirement for "generic" (non-purebred) tigers. Buying Tony the Tiger is not just for breakfast anymore.

Progress is indeed being made in this arena. A little over a month ago, a judge in East Baton Rouge (La.) District Court ruled that Tiger Truck Stop, owned by Michael Sandlin, has seen its last permit to keep Tony, a 550-pound Siberian-Bengal tiger, on display. The national, nonprofit Animal Legal Defense Fund, which spearheaded the effort to free Tony, reported that although the court did not revoke the current permit, it did issue a permanent injunction preventing the Louisiana Department of Wildlife and Fisheries from renewing the permit again come December. Without question, the "unhealthy and unnatural environment of a truck stop" is not a suitable habitat for a tiger or any animal. As a result, Tony, who has lived at the Tiger Truck Stop in Grosse Tete, Louisiana for the past decade, will finally be headed for a new home. In addition, Massachusetts School of Law (MSL), which boasts one of the oldest and premier animal rights programs of any law school in the country, is taking a lead role in helping these noble animals. Following is just a partial list of our efforts:

- On Monday, July 25, 2011, Rose Church, an MSL alumna, will be spearheading a conference at the International Fund for Animal Welfare Office in Washington, D.C., which we will be attending along with other experts and major animal advocacy groups. The purpose is to discuss the current captive tiger problem, determine solutions, and draft ap-

propriate legislation. Confirmed attendees for the meeting include The World Wildlife Fund; Global Federation of Animal Sanctuaries, Born Free USA; Wild Cat Conservation Legal Aid Society; Animal Legal Defense Fund; U.S. Humane Society; the Ian Somerhalder Foundation; World Council for Animal Rights, Inc.; and Big Cat Rescue.
- We have been in contact with the office of U.S. Senator John Kerry (D-MA) to see if he will sponsor a bill addressing the problem.
- Attorney Christopher A. Leverone, an MSL alumnus and associate at the Law Offices of Bruce A. Bierhans, LLC, has been working on gaining political support for this initiative within the Commonwealth of Massachusetts.
- We will be meeting on a weekly basis with current MSL students, who will be conducting legal research on current bills, drafting legislation, and fact gathering.
- We are also working to schedule a meeting with the USDA to get agreement on banning the practice of allowing the eight- to 12-week petting loophole, and the U.S. Fish and Wildlife Service to reinstitute the permit requirement for cross-bred tigers.

No private citizen should need a captive tiger as a backyard pet; there is no justifiable reason for doing so. Tigers should live in the wild or in well-maintained, accredited sanctuaries, not kept in unlit trailers (during the exhibitions) or cages that are too small for them to do anything but turn around. The breeding, sale, and trade of tigers need to be banned completely, beginning with the eight- to 12-week petting loophole, which serves no purpose other than to make money for those who cruelly mistreat the cubs. For our government to endorse this is ignorant, deplorable, and shameful.

#

APPENDIX

ABOUT THE AUTHORS

Diane Sullivan is an Assistant Dean and Professor at the Massachusetts School of Law in Andover, and also serves as director of the school's Animal Rights Program. Reach her at dianes@mslaw.edu. Holly Vietzke is an Assistant Professor at the school and is co-director of the Animal Rights program. Reach her at holly@mslaw.edu. Rose Church is a graduate of the Massachusetts School of Law and CEO of World Council For Animal Rights, Inc.

Diane and Apollo

APPENDIX

The true healing power of Apollo
By Diane M. Sullivan (2017)

Hasten up! Apollo sits beside my bed and barks. It may be a new year, but it is still 4 a.m. When I don't respond, he barks again. The next time even louder. I get up. Really, what choice do I have?

There are days when Apollo comes to wake me that I think I cannot rise. Apollo will have none of my refusal. He will insist I get up, sometimes jumping on the bed to put his face to mine. "Let's go. Get up! Why are you still sleeping?" And so I get up!

Trying to stand is painful at first. I don't feel well, but this is of no consequence to Apollo. It is as if he says, "you need to keep moving," and he is correct. Besides, he wants his walk so out the door we go. He is in search of squirrels and rabbits to bark at insanely. I am in search of another sunrise. We are both grateful for the day. I recall our first walk. I ended up lassoed in his leash, and had to sit by the side of the road to free myself.

Apollo comes from a harsh past no dog should have endured. But now he has me, his servant. We walk where Apollo wants to go but he carries me through darkness, into the light of another day.

When Apollo first arrived he would roll in water, taking a mud bath at every opportunity -- today, he refuses to step on the grass if it is at all wet. If we go out and it is even sprinkling, he turns and barks at me as if I have the power to magically close the sky.

Yet, as entitled as Apollo has become, he stands ready to protect me.

In under a second he will rise to full alert and likely defend me with his life. Often before the walk ends he will throw himself onto the ground, usually in the middle of the road refusing to

Life's Not Always a Day at the Beach

stand and walk. Traffic will be halted and he seems to be smirking at me as I try to get him up. Often times someone will yell, "that is a really beautiful dog." I will respond that he's not a dog, but a monster. "You love him anyway, don't you?" the person will ask. "Would I be out walking him at 4:15 a.m. if I didn't," I retort. Suddenly he will jump up and take me back home.

When it is time for me to leave for a day of work, I will tell him that I love him. I will cross my fingers and tell him to be a good boy. He will tilt his head as he listens. At this moment, he is adorable. I am grateful he is a part of my life. How far we have come from his first months of adoption when he destroyed everything in sight, including eating the arms off the sofa and living room chair.

When I return home at 5 p.m., usually to take care of him between my law classes, he runs to greet me. No one before has ever greeted me with his kind of enthusiasm; except maybe his predecessor, my chow chow dog Winnie. He will want his evening walk without delay. Patience is not his strong suit. It isn't mine, either. Apollo sees life as an adventure. I am learning too.

I go inside my home with trepidation. In December, I put up the Christmas tree and all the decorations, something I refrained from doing the previous year for fear of Apollo's destruction. I envisioned the tree down, decorations smashed entirely, and Apollo wrapped up in lights. After work, to my astonishment, everything was intact.

Now as we start another year, it's clear that Apollo has settled into my home, his home -- our home. I don't know what the days ahead will bring, but thankfully we're together and I've realized that Apollo came to me not to be rescued, but to rescue me.

I Rescued Two Dogs: Now Who Will Rescue Me?

By Diane M. Sullivan
with Amy Dimitriadis
and Kathryn Villare

Is a daily account of two rescue dogs as they settle into their new home. The author, Diane M. Sullivan, Assistant Dean at the Massachusetts School of Law, rescued two chow chow puppies after her 14-year-old chow Winnie passed away. Apollo and Sasha are the stars of this new book, who day after day find new ways to cause mayhem and destruction at home, in the park, in the street, or the hiking trail.

Page after page is filled with actual accounts and photographs of the hilarious antics of two adorable, mischievous puppies growing into adorable, mischievous adults.
You won't want to put this page-turner down.

All proceeds from the sale of this book benefit The Shadow Fund NE

Available at The Shadow Fund NE Website: http://shadowfundne.org/, Amazon, and Barnes and Noble.